What People Are Saying about Threshold Bible Study

"This remarkable series provides a method of study and reflection that is bound to produce rich fruit." ▨ **DIANNE BERGANT, C.S.A.**, *Catholic Theological Union, Chicago*

"This fine series will provide needed tools that can deepen your understanding of Scripture, but most importantly it can deepen your faith."
▨ **MOST REVEREND CHARLES J. CHAPUT, O.F.M. CAP.**, *Archbishop of Philadelphia*

"*Threshold Bible Study* is a wonderful series that helps modern people read the Bible with insight and joy."
▨ **RICHARD J. CLIFFORD, S.J.**, *Boston College School of Theology and Ministry*

"This is a wonderful gift for those wishing to make a home for the Word in their hearts."
▨ **CAROL J. DEMPSEY, OP**, *University of Portland, OR*

"Written in a sprightly easy-to-understand style, these volumes will engage the mind, heart, and spirit."
▨ **ALEXANDER A. DI LELLA, O.F.M.**, *The Catholic University of America*

"By covering a wide variety of themes and topics, Threshold Bible Study continually breathes new life into ancient texts."
▨ **JOHN R. DONAHUE, S.J.**, *St. Mary's Seminary and University*

"*Threshold Bible Study* offers a marvelous new approach for individuals and groups to study themes in our rich biblical and theological tradition."
▨ **JOHN ENDRES, S.J.**, *Jesuit School of Theology, Berkeley*

"*Threshold Bible Study* offers you an encounter with the Word that will make your heart come alive." ▨ **TIM GRAY**, *President of the Augustine Institute, Denver*

"*Threshold Bible Study* offers solid scholarship and spiritual depth."
▨ **SCOTT HAHN**, *Franciscan University of Steubenville*

DIVINE
MERCY

Stephen J. Binz

TWENTY
THIRD
PUBLICATIONS
www.23rdpublications.com

TWENTY-THIRD PUBLICATIONS
A Division of Bayard
One Montauk Avenue, Suite 200
New London, CT 06320
(860) 437-3012 or (800) 321-0411
www.23rdpublications.com

SECOND PRINTING 2016

ISBN: 978-1-82785-114-5
Library of Congress Control Number: 2015952049
Printed in the U.S.A.

Contents

LESSONS 13-18

LESSONS 19-24

LESSONS 25-30

How to Use
Threshold Bible Study

Each book in the Threshold Bible Study series is designed to lead you through a new doorway of biblical awareness, to accompany you across a unique threshold of understanding. The characters, places, and images that you encounter in each of these topical studies will help you explore fresh dimensions of your faith and discover richer insights for your spiritual life.

Threshold Bible Study covers biblical themes in depth in a short amount of time. Unlike more traditional Bible studies that treat a biblical book or series of books, Threshold Bible Study aims to address specific topics within the entire Bible. The goal is not for you to comprehend everything about each passage, but rather for you to understand what a variety of passages from different books of the Bible reveals about the topic of each study.

Threshold Bible Study offers you an opportunity to explore the entire Bible from the viewpoint of a variety of different themes. The commentary that follows each biblical passage launches your reflection about that passage and helps you begin to see its significance within the context of your contemporary experience. The questions following the commentary challenge you to understand the passage more fully and apply it to your own life. The prayer starter helps conclude your study by integrating learning into your relationship with God.

These studies are designed for maximum flexibility. Each study is presented in a workbook format, with sections for reading, reflecting, writing, discussing, and praying. Space for writing after each question is ideal for personal study and allows group members to prepare in advance for their discussion.

The thirty lessons in each topic may be used by an individual over the period of a month, or by a group for six sessions, with lessons to be studied each week before the next group meeting. These studies are ideal for Bible study groups, small Christian communities, adult faith formation, student groups, Sunday school, neighborhood groups, and family reading, as well as for individual learning.

The method of Threshold Bible Study is rooted in the classical tradition of *lectio divina*, an ancient yet contemporary means for reading the Scriptures reflectively and prayerfully. Reading and interpreting the text (*lectio*) is followed by reflective meditation on its message (*meditatio*). This reading and reflecting flows into prayer from the heart (*oratio* and *contemplatio*).

This ancient method assures us that Bible study is a matter of both the mind and the heart. It is not just an intellectual exercise to learn more and be able to discuss the Bible with others. It is, more importantly, a transforming experience. Reflecting on God's word, guided by the Holy Spirit, illumines the mind with wisdom and stirs the heart with zeal.

Following the personal Bible study, Threshold Bible Study offers a method for extending *lectio divina* into a weekly conversation with a small group. This communal experience will allow participants to enhance their appreciation of the message and build up a spiritual community (*collatio*). The end result will be to increase not only individual faith but also faithful witness in the context of daily life (*operatio*).

Through the spiritual disciplines of Scripture reading, study, reflection, conversation, and prayer, you will experience God's grace more abundantly as your life is rooted more deeply in Christ. The risen Jesus said: "Listen! I am standing at the door, knocking; if you hear my voice and open the door, I will come in to you and eat with you, and you with me" (Rev 3:20). Listen to the Word of God, open the door, and cross the threshold to an unimaginable dwelling with God!

SUGGESTIONS FOR INDIVIDUAL STUDY

- Make your Bible reading a time of prayer. Ask for God's guidance as you read the Scriptures.

- Try to study daily, or as often as possible according to the circumstances of your life.

- Read the Bible passage carefully, trying to understand both its meaning and its personal application as you read. Some persons find it helpful to read the passage aloud.

- Read the passage in another Bible translation. Each version adds to your understanding of the original text.

- Allow the commentary to help you comprehend and apply the scriptural text. The commentary is only a beginning, not the last word, on the meaning of the passage.

- After reflecting on each question, write out your responses. The very act of writing will help you clarify your thoughts, bring new insights, and amplify your understanding.

- As you reflect on your answers, think about how you can live God's word in the context of your daily life.

- Conclude each daily lesson by reading the prayer and continuing with your own prayer from the heart.

- Make sure your reflections and prayers are matters of both the mind and the heart. A true encounter with God's word is always a transforming experience.

- Choose a word or a phrase from the lesson to carry with you throughout the day as a reminder of your encounter with God's life-changing word.

- Share your learning experience with at least one other person whom you trust for additional insights and affirmation. The ideal way to share learning is in a small group that meets regularly.

SUGGESTIONS FOR GROUP STUDY

- Meet regularly; weekly is ideal. Try to be on time and make attendance a high priority for the sake of the group. The average group meets for about an hour.

- Open each session with a prepared prayer, a song, or a reflection. Find some appropriate way to bring the group from the workaday world into a sacred time of graced sharing.

- If you have not been together before, name tags are very helpful as a group begins to become acquainted with the other group members.

- Spend the first session getting acquainted with one another, reading the Introduction aloud, and discussing the questions that follow.

- Appoint a group facilitator to provide guidance to the discussion. The role of facilitator may rotate among members each week. The facilitator simply keeps the discussion on track; each person shares responsibility for the group. There is no need for the facilitator to be a trained teacher.

- Try to study the six lessons on your own during the week. When you have done your own reflection and written your own answers, you will be better prepared to discuss the six scriptural lessons with the group. If you have not had an opportunity to study the passages during the week, meet with the group anyway to share support and insights.

- Participate in the discussion as much as you are able, offering your thoughts, insights, feelings, and decisions. You learn by sharing with others the fruits of your study.

- Be careful not to dominate the discussion. It is important that everyone in the group be offered an equal opportunity to share the results of their work. Try to link what you say to the comments of others so that the group remains on the topic.

- When discussing your own personal thoughts or feelings, use "I" language. Be as personal and honest as appropriate and be very cautious about giving advice to others.

- Listen attentively to the other members of the group so as to learn from their insights. The words of the Bible affect each person in a different way, so a group provides a wealth of understanding for each member.

- Don't fear silence. Silence in a group is as important as silence in personal study. It allows individuals time to listen to the voice of God's Spirit and the opportunity to form their thoughts before they speak.

- Solicit several responses for each question. The thoughts of different people will build on the answers of others and will lead to deeper insights for all.

- Don't fear controversy. Differences of opinions are a sign of a healthy and honest group. If you cannot resolve an issue, continue on, agreeing to disagree. There is probably some truth in each viewpoint.

- Discuss the questions that seem most important for the group. There is no need to cover all the questions in the group session.

- Realize that some questions about the Bible cannot be resolved, even by experts. Don't get stuck on some issue for which there are no clear answers.

- Whatever is said in the group is said in confidence and should be regarded as such.

- Pray as a group in whatever way feels comfortable. Pray for the members of your group throughout the week.

Schedule for Group Study

SESSION 1: INTRODUCTION   DATE: _____

SESSION 2: LESSONS 1-6   DATE: _____

SESSION 3: LESSONS 7-12   DATE: _____

SESSION 4: LESSONS 13-18   DATE: _____

SESSION 5: LESSONS 19-24   DATE: _____

SESSION 6: LESSONS 25-30   DATE: _____

You, O Lord, are a God merciful and gracious, slow to anger and abounding in steadfast love and faithfulness. PS 86:15

Divine Mercy

God's mercy is the core of biblical revelation and the expression of God's own heart. When we study the Bible—both the Old and New Testaments—we discover that God's most fundamental attribute is mercy. The God revealed in Scripture suffers with his creatures and has a heart for the poor and the lost.

An abstract and philosophical notion of God describes God as infinite, eternal, almighty, and all-knowing. This understanding of the divine being seems awfully distant from the personal situations and real life of people. When God is conceived so apathetically, it is difficult to imagine much divine empathy for the struggles of human life. Such a God seems alien and ultimately irrelevant in a world with such pressing problems.

But God's historical self-revelation, as understood through the tradition of ancient Israel and the Christian church, presents quite different divine characteristics. This merciful God does not tire of seeking out his beloved ones. God cares deeply about the plight of his people and shows deep compassion in their suffering. When God's people are unfaithful, God responds to their rejection with a merciful love that they will never merit or deserve. Again and again, God demonstrates faithful love for the world and calls people to a joyful and abundant life.

Reflection and Discussion

- In what sense is mercy revealed in Scripture as God's most essential quality?

- Why is it important that God be revealed as both almighty and merciful?

Mercy in Salvation History

There is a false but widely held opinion that the God of the Old Testament is a vengeful and angry God, while the God of the New Testament is a gracious and merciful God. But in reality, both testaments reveal the same God, who is revealed through words and deeds of mercy. Throughout the history of salvation, God's mercy creates and sustains life. Mercy is the divine power that continually protects, promotes, builds up, and creates life anew.

The opening verses of the Bible testify that the creation of the world and its creatures is not the result of some inherent right to exist, but of God's desire to extend divine love. When alienation from God led to human hostility toward nature and other people, God did not abandon the world to its fate but enacted countermeasures to prevent humanity from running into disaster and falling into misery. With great mercy, God made a new beginning with the call of Abraham and promised blessings for all the people of the earth. God does not resist evil with force and violence, but over and over again, God creates new life and blessings.

The Old Testament message of mercy is not simply a spiritual message; it is a message with a physically concrete and social dimension that is essential to it.

When God saw the suffering of his people in Egypt and heard their cries, God came down to liberate and redeem them. This is not an indifferent God who sits obliviously on a heavenly throne, nor is this a rash and vengeful God who responds from afar. The God described in Israel's Torah is merciful and gracious, slow to anger and abounding in faithful love. With a heart full of mercy, God intervenes on behalf of slaves, offering them freedom and abundant life.

God demonstrates divine mercy throughout the history of ancient Israel. God's people merited death because of continual transgression, rebellion, and sin. But God, through divine mercy, grants them space for living anew. Biblical history testifies that God takes no satisfaction from the death of the sinner but finds delight when the sinner repents and continues to live.

But we must also understand that the revelation of God as merciful has nothing to do with false familiarity. God is not a chummy companion who is lax toward evil and overlooks our sin. Rather, the truth of God's mercy is indissolubly bound up with the revelation of divine holiness, with God's sovereignty and superiority over everything earthly. God is totally transcendent, yet condescends to draw near to creation.

The message of God's mercy does not stand in opposition to God's justice. The manifestations of God's justice in Israel's history and the assurance of universal divine justice gave hope to the people. Evidence of justice in an unjust world is already a work of mercy for the oppressed and those whose rights have been denied. So the message of God's mercy is not a message of cheap grace. God expects the Israelites to do what is right and just in imitation of God's own nature.

Because of God's holiness, God must offer resistance to evil. In the Bible this resistance is revealed as the wrath or judgment of God. We may dislike this depiction of God, yet divine wrath does not imply angry responses and emotionally surging rage. Wrath is God's resistance to malice and injustice. It is God's dynamic expression of his holiness in the face of evil. On the basis of God's holiness, God can't do anything other than punish evil and reward good. For this reason, mercy does not stand in opposition to the message of justice. Only a God who stands above and not under the demands of pure justice can forgive and pardon. God demonstrates divine sovereignty above all in forgiving and pardoning.

In his mercy, God holds back his justified wrath. God delays divine judgment. He does this in order to provide people the opportunity for conversion. Divine mercy grants sinners a period of grace and desires their conversion. Mercy is ultimately grace for conversion.

In speaking of God's mercy, the Old Testament most often employs one of two different Hebrew words. The most frequently used term is *hesed*. It means unmerited favor, divine grace, and mercy. It is God's free and gracious turning toward his people with loving kindness. *Hesed* flows from God's relationship with Israel, the covenant God established with them. Because of this relationship, God's mercy is faithful love.

But since a relationship is a two-way bond, it seems according to human understanding that faithful love no longer obliges when Israel breaks the covenant and no longer respects its conditions. But here, God's mercy reveals its deeper aspects as love that continues giving, a love more powerful than betrayal, a grace stronger than sin. God, who is all-powerful and all-holy, concerns himself with the self-caused distresses of his people, hears their laments and bends down to them in their needs, and despite their infidelity, continues to care, to forgive, and to offer another chance, despite their deserved just punishment. This is divine mercy. It exceeds human experience and transcends human imagination.

The other frequently occurring Hebrew word for mercy is *rahamin*. It designates tender compassion and deeply felt care. Its root, *rehem*, means "a mother's womb." Thus, the term expresses a maternal love that arises from an original bond and unity. The recipient of this tender love can do nothing to deserve or merit it. *Rahamin* arises, we might say, from the necessity of the heart. As a maternal instinct, it suggests patient understanding, protection from danger, and a readiness to forgive.

In summary, the message of God's mercy permeates the entire Old Testament. This divine mercy is the organizing center of God's many other attributes: holiness, justice, fidelity, graciousness, patience, forbearance, condescension, and generosity. God comes to the aid of those who are lost and held in bondage. He is the protector of the poor and those without a voice. Again and again, God restrains his just and holy wrath and shows mercy to his unfaithful people, offering them another opportunity for repentance and conversion. Mercy is the externally visible feature of the divine heart, the effective aspect of God's very essence.

Reflection and Discussion

- What part of the Old Testament most convinces me that God is merciful and not vengeful?

- What is the biblical understanding of divine wrath? How can I reconcile God's just wrath with divine mercy?

Mercy Embodied in Jesus Christ

The incarnation, ministry, death, and resurrection of Jesus Christ are the supreme expression of God's mercy. Each account of healing, exorcism, and forgiveness by Jesus in the gospels is a cameo of divine mercy. In Jesus, God's mercy is extended to the afflicted, the poor, the needy, and the sinners of Israel. Through his public ministry, the primary facets of God's mercy are given a tangible and personal shape. The mercy of Jesus expresses itself in the inclusion of social outcasts in his company, the forgiveness of repentant sinners, the healing of those sick in mind and body, acknowledgment of the needs of the poor, compassion for tired and hungry crowds, and even pardon for those who violently put him to death.

Jesus' demonstration of divine mercy in individual acts throughout the gospels illustrates the redemption that God extends to the whole world through the sacrificial death and resurrection of his Son. The God of mercy has desired the salvation of all people from all eternity. In the cross of Jesus Christ, the mercy of God stands as a sign over the world, over history, and over every human life. In the mercy revealed on the cross, God's power is most clearly displayed.

God does not sit enthroned in majesty over the world, apathetic to the grief and sufferings that fill it. God became human in Jesus Christ so that divine mercy may be felt and expressed as tangible compassion, through a literal suffering with humanity. In the divine incarnation of God's Son, God voluntarily surrendered himself to suffering and death. In the humanity of Jesus, God wills to suffer with us and for us. So, in all our suffering we are joined by the one who experiences and carries that suffering with us. And because the divine Christ, who is immortal and Lord over life and death, suffered and died, he conquered death and restored life.

In the crucifixion of Christ, God expresses divine mercy in the most extravagant way. On the cross, God gives himself completely, the greatest self-gift imaginable. In pouring out his life for us completely, even unto death, God gives to the world the fullest expression of merciful love. When we look to the cross, we can see love to the full, compassion in its most tangible form, and divine mercy to the upmost.

The teachings and actions of Jesus demonstrate that the loneliness, pain, and grief that humans feel—and to which God's mercy is directed—are rooted in humanity's distance from God. But God desires to have us close, to bestow his nearness on us in our adversity. God's mercy, therefore, is directed to our happiness and fulfillment. Divine mercy expands our hearts, offers us hope, restores serenity and peace, and gives us the experience of inner blessedness.

Although God offers everyone the saving effects of his merciful love, we must open our lives to receive it in order to experience its transforming power. Although God desires that his love be reciprocated, God does not force our response or bypass our freedom. We can ignore or reject God's mercy because God treats human freedom with radical seriousness. Our salvation depends on our decision and our response to the offer of God's love. God urges but does not force; he pursues but does not overpower or subdue.

In his mercy, God holds the possibility of salvation open for all human beings who are willing to allow their heart to be changed, even if their guilt is ever so great and their former life ever so messed up. Every person is able to trust in the immeasurable mercy of God. A person's "no" of refusal is always weak alongside the unconditional "yes" that God has spoken to humanity in the death and resurrection of Christ. In ways unfathomable to us, God never ceases to court human beings to the very end of life. God even enlists the intercession of all the angels and saints of heaven on behalf of every individual so that we might choose eternal life over the rejection that results in unending death.

There is a place for everyone under the mantle of God's mercy. Jesus Christ as judge of the living and the dead is, indeed, the one who has died for all on the cross. The biblical message of mercy assures us that he is a gracious judge. In the salvation of the world, divine mercy has the first as well as the last word. The mercy embodied in Jesus Christ is the uplifting, hope-inducing message on which we can rely in every situation, both in life and in death. It is our refuge, our comfort, and the source of our confidence.

Reflection and Discussion

- In what sense can it be said that mercy is the heart of the gospel?

- In what ways do I experience God having mercy on me and on the whole world?

Works of Mercy as Our Response and Responsibility

The experience of divine mercy encourages and obliges us to become witnesses of mercy ourselves. If God treats us mercifully and forgives us, then we too must forgive and show mercy to one another. In our acts of mercy, God's mercy for our neighbor becomes concretely realized. These acts of witnessing mercy to others have been traditionally categorized as seven spiritual works and seven corporal works of mercy.

The spiritual works of mercy are acts of compassion by which we help others with their emotional and spiritual needs. These seven are the following: converting sinners, instructing the ignorant, advising the doubtful, comforting the sorrowful, bearing wrongs patiently, forgiving injuries, and praying for the living and dead. These works are a kind of preventive medicine for the spiritual poverty of shame, doubt, and despair. This kind of poverty drains life of all energy, joy, and sense of purpose, and it is the kind of poverty that can last forever.

The corporal works of mercy are compassionate deeds by which we help others with their material and physical needs. These seven are the following: feeding the hungry, sheltering the homeless, clothing the naked, visiting the sick, visiting the imprisoned, giving drink to the thirsty, and burying the dead. The message of divine mercy is not a theory that is alien to reality, nor does it stop at the level of sentimental expressions of pity. Jesus teaches us to be merciful like God: "Be merciful, just as your Father is merciful" (Luke 6:36).

In the Letter to the Ephesians, we read: "Therefore be imitators of God, as beloved children, and live in love, as Christ loved us and gave himself up for us, a fragrant offering and sacrifice to God" (Eph 5:1-2). This pattern of *imitatio Dei*, the imitation of God and his actions in Jesus Christ, is foundational for the Bible. Therefore, the message of divine mercy has consequences for the life of every Christian, for the pastoral praxis of the church, and for the contributions that Christians should render to the humane, just, and merciful structuring of society.

Jesus' family is worldwide, and his brothers and sisters include all who are in need of life's basic necessities: food, hospitality, clothing, health care, education, counseling, prayer, pardon, and companionship. The radical love of neighbor that Jesus demands is possible for us only because we have first received the love of God in the form of divine mercy. Only by imitating God in his gift of mercy to the world can we make talk about God's mercy credible and persuasive; only in this way can we make it a message of hope for the world.

Reflection and Discussion

- Why does Scripture describe our works of mercy as an imitation of God?

- In what sense are works of mercy both a response and a responsibility for us?

Prayer

Creating and Redeeming God, you have manifested your presence in the world through your unfailing mercy. We praise you for the ways you have shown your faithful and compassionate love to the world. During this study, teach me the many ways your mercy has transformed the world and how I can respond to your faithful love through works of mercy. Send your Holy Spirit upon me to guide, encourage, and enlighten me as I read and contemplate your inspired word.

SUGGESTIONS FOR FACILITATORS, GROUP SESSION 1

1. If the group is meeting for the first time, or if there are newcomers joining the group, it is helpful to provide nametags.

2. Distribute the books to the members of the group.

3. You may want to ask the participants to introduce themselves and tell the group a bit about themselves.

4. Ask one or more of these introductory questions:
   - What drew you to join this group?
   - What is your biggest fear in beginning this Bible study?

5. You may want to pray this prayer as a group:
   Come upon us, Holy Spirit, to enlighten and guide us as we begin this study of divine mercy. You inspired the biblical authors to express the mercy of God as manifested to the people of Israel and most fully in the life of Jesus. Now stir our minds and our hearts to deepen our understanding and experience of divine mercy and to express mercy to people in need. Motivate us to read the Scriptures, and give us a deeper love for God's word each day. Bless us during this session and throughout the coming week with the fire of your love.

6. Read the Introduction aloud, pausing at each question for discussion. Group members may wish to write the insights of the group as each question is discussed. Encourage several members of the group to respond to each question.

7. Don't feel compelled to finish the complete Introduction during the session. It is better to allow sufficient time to talk about the questions raised than to rush to the end. Group members may read any remaining sections on their own after the group meeting.

8. Instruct group members to read the first six lessons on their own during the six days before the next group meeting. They should write out their own answers to the questions as preparation for next week's group discussion.

9. Fill in the date for each group meeting under "Schedule for Group Study."

10. Conclude by praying aloud together the prayer at the end of the Introduction.

"I have observed the misery of my people who are in Egypt; I have heard their cry on account of their taskmasters. Indeed, I know their sufferings." EXOD 3:7

God Has Ears for the Afflicted

EXODUS 2:23–3:15 ²³*After a long time the king of Egypt died. The Israelites groaned under their slavery, and cried out. Out of the slavery their cry for help rose up to God.* ²⁴*God heard their groaning, and God remembered his covenant with Abraham, Isaac, and Jacob.* ²⁵*God looked upon the Israelites, and God took notice of them.*

3 ¹*Moses was keeping the flock of his father-in-law Jethro, the priest of Midian; he led his flock beyond the wilderness, and came to Horeb, the mountain of God.* ²*There the angel of the Lord appeared to him in a flame of fire out of a bush; he looked, and the bush was blazing, yet it was not consumed.* ³*Then Moses said, "I must turn aside and look at this great sight, and see why the bush is not burned up."* ⁴*When the Lord saw that he had turned aside to see, God called to him out of the bush, "Moses, Moses!" And he said, "Here I am."* ⁵*Then he said, "Come no closer! Remove the sandals from your feet, for the place on which you are standing is holy ground."* ⁶*He said further, "I am the God of your father, the God of Abraham, the God of Isaac, and the God of Jacob." And Moses hid his face, for he was afraid to look at God.*

⁷*Then the Lord said, "I have observed the misery of my people who are in Egypt; I have heard their cry on account of their taskmasters. Indeed, I know their sufferings,* ⁸*and I have come down to deliver them from the Egyptians, and to bring them up out of that land to a good and broad land, a land flowing with milk and honey, to*

the country of the Canaanites, the Hittites, the Amorites, the Perizzites, the Hivites, and the Jebusites. ⁹The cry of the Israelites has now come to me; I have also seen how the Egyptians oppress them. ¹⁰So come, I will send you to Pharaoh to bring my people, the Israelites, out of Egypt." ¹¹But Moses said to God, "Who am I that I should go to Pharaoh, and bring the Israelites out of Egypt?" ¹²He said, "I will be with you; and this shall be the sign for you that it is I who sent you: when you have brought the people out of Egypt, you shall worship God on this mountain."

¹³But Moses said to God, "If I come to the Israelites and say to them, 'The God of your ancestors has sent me to you,' and they ask me, 'What is his name?' what shall I say to them?" ¹⁴God said to Moses, "I AM WHO I AM." He said further, "Thus you shall say to the Israelites, 'I AM has sent me to you.'" ¹⁵God also said to Moses, "Thus you shall say to the Israelites, 'The Lord, the God of your ancestors, the God of Abraham, the God of Isaac, and the God of Jacob, has sent me to you':

This is my name forever,
and this my title for all generations."

Throughout the Scriptures of Israel, God is identified as the God who brought his people out of their slavery in Egypt and entered into a personal relationship with them. This act of divine liberation began as God heard the groaning and cries of the Israelites as they labored under the cruel oppression of their taskmasters. God then looked upon the Israelites and observed their misery. God's closeness to the people is manifested in direct, first-person speech: I have observed, I have heard, I know, I have come down (verses 7-8). When God said, "I know their sufferings," God was not speaking about some information he had attained from a distant source. Rather, God has a personal concern for this people and cares for them. For God to "know" suffering means that the suffering has entered into the divine being so that God suffers with the people. This is a living God, who attends to human misery, has a heart for the afflicted ones, and with divine mercy begins to act on their behalf. This merciful God intervenes, liberates, and redeems.

God's decision to "come down to deliver" the Israelites from their bondage was a personal action. Not only did God free this oppressed people from slavery, but God also enters into a personal relationship with them, joining them in covenant. God's relationship to the Israelites was rooted in the covenant with

Abraham, Isaac, and Jacob. But God's manifestation to Israel's ancestors had been many generations ago. Now, God would manifest the divine presence to Moses, and then to the whole people, joining them all in a divine relationship.

The revelation of God's name is a key aspect of God's personal action for the Israelites. "I AM WHO I AM" in Hebrew does not at all imply a static, unchanging existence, as it later came to imply in the Greek language. When the Hebrew Bible was translated into Greek in around 200 BC in Alexandria, the revelation of God's name was interpreted in the sense of the Greek philosophy of being. Accordingly, the name of God was translated as "I am the one who is." But the name in Hebrew does not simply mean "to exist" but concretely means "to be present there," and, in fact, to be there with and for others.

The divine name enunciates God's innermost reality: God's being is divine presence with and for his people. This is not a God who can be tied down or captured in a name or an image. God's name conveys the reality that this personal God will be with the Israelites in their distress and will accompany them on their way. God will hear their cries and answer their pleas. God's name, therefore, is both a commitment and a promise.

The revelation of God's name, as being present for and with his people in response to their groans and cries, suggests that God's essential nature on our behalf is mercy. And this mercy is not a distant, impersonal handout. God's mercy is present, self-revealing, and oriented toward personal relationship. God "comes down" to free us from oppression and our slavery to sin. But God's mercy wants to do even more for us. God desires to give us the greatest gift we are capable of receiving. This divine gift is union with God; it is ultimately, as the New Testament reveals, sharing in the divine nature. God descended to share our life so that we could ascend to share in divine life.

Yet, this revelation of God who descends to draw near to his people is not a close acquaintance or a false familiarity. God is revealed in a fire that does not consume, telling Moses to remove his sandals, for the ground of their encounter is holy. Moses hid his face and is unable to look upon God. While God's self-revelation is the essence of mercy, God remains the all-holy one. God's mercy is indissolubly bound up with God's indescribable sovereignty. This God of mercy has qualities of both transcendence and immanence: God is holy and personal, distant and close, above the earth and descending to be present with people in need.

Reflection and Discussion

- What does God's self-revelation to Moses at the burning bush make known to me about divine mercy?

- God said to Moses, "I know their sufferings, and I have come down to deliver them." How did the Israelites experience God in this way? How do I experience God in this way?

- In what ways does the church's worship of God express both divine transcendence and immanence? Is God more sovereign or familiar in my personal prayer? Why is it important to maintain both?

Prayer

God of our ancestors, you look upon the misery of your people and you hear their cries in distress. Look upon me with mercy and listen to my prayer today. I trust in your personal care and compassion for me.

"The Lord, the Lord, a God merciful and gracious, slow to anger, and abounding in steadfast love and faithfulness." EXOD 34:6

A God Rich in Mercy

EXODUS 34:4-9 ⁴*So Moses cut two tablets of stone like the former ones; and he rose early in the morning and went up on Mount Sinai, as the Lord had commanded him, and took in his hand the two tablets of stone. ⁵The Lord descended in the cloud and stood with him there, and proclaimed the name, "The Lord." ⁶The Lord passed before him, and proclaimed,*

"The Lord, the Lord,
a God merciful and gracious,
slow to anger,
and abounding in steadfast love and faithfulness,
⁷keeping steadfast love for the thousandth generation,
forgiving iniquity and transgression and sin,
yet by no means clearing the guilty,
but visiting the iniquity of the parents
upon the children
and the children's children,
to the third and the fourth generation."

⁸And Moses quickly bowed his head toward the earth, and worshiped. ⁹He said, "If now I have found favor in your sight, O Lord, I pray, let the Lord go with us. Although this is a stiff-necked people, pardon our iniquity and our sin, and take us for your inheritance."

S hortly after God's people had been liberated from slavery and entered into covenant with God at Mount Sinai, they became unfaithful and sinned against the Lord. While Moses was with God on the mountain for forty days, the people below experienced the time as an intolerable delay. The Israelites displayed a serious act of disloyalty to God by erecting and worshiping an idol in the form of a golden calf. God's just anger flared, and Moses shattered the tablets of the covenant at the foot of the mountain as a sign that, from his point of view, the covenant had been terminated.

But when everything appeared to be lost, Moses pleaded for the Israelites, and his persuasive arguments led to the amazing reversal of God's intentions. God's ability to be persuaded demonstrates that the divine nature is not static, unchanging being but is, rather, personal, totally free, and responsive to the changing needs of a vital relationship with people. God pronounced the divine name again and said to Moses, "I will be gracious to whom I will be gracious, and I will show mercy on whom I will show mercy" (33:19). God cannot be limited to any human understanding of just compensation. So God commands Moses to prepare two tablets for writing the words of the covenant and to again ascend Mount Sinai. Despite the people's sinful infidelity, God does not let them fall into ruin but gives them another opportunity to be covenant partners.

God descended in a cloud to meet Moses on the mountain and gave him a new revelation of the divine name and the divine nature. God is "merciful and gracious," "slow to anger," "abounding in steadfast love and faithfulness," and having steadfast love that extends hundreds of times farther than his just punishments (verses 6-7). The word translated "merciful" comes from a Hebrew word whose root means "womb." The word connotes the compassion of a mother for the child in her womb. The word translated "steadfast love" is often translated as "mercy." It implies both tenacious fidelity to a relationship and unrelenting love. It describes God's constant and tender love for Israel as God's children, and it expresses God's absolute resolve to continue in loving commitment to those who share the relationship of covenant.

As in God's revelation to Moses at the burning bush, this association of God's name and God's nature indicates that mercy is an essential expression of God's sovereignty, freedom, and fidelity. Mercy is at the heart of Israel's central affirmation of the essence of their God. By acting with mercy, God is not only faithful to the Israelites despite their infidelity but also faithful to himself and his own divine name.

This declaration of God's nature—proclaiming that God is gracious, merciful, faithful, forgiving, and just—is repeated throughout the Old Testament, especially in the psalms. Its proclamation of God's gracious and merciful essence is not a speculative statement or a poetic description of God; rather, it is a statement of faith based on God's own historical self-revelation. In fact, God's mercy is most manifest in dealing with the repeated sins of the Israelites. Divine mercy is shown precisely to those who do not deserve it. This formula, in fact, serves as the summary of God's self-definition in the Old Testament. It became the primary way that God was addressed and announced in Israel's public liturgy.

Reflection and Discussion

- Verses 6-7 are the heart of the Old Testament. What is astonishing about the way the Israelites describe their belief in God?

- After God's self-revelation of the divine nature, Moses could only bow his head to the ground in worship. How do I respond to God's merciful love in my worship and prayer?

Prayer

Lord our God, you are merciful, gracious, and filled with committed love.
As I bow in your presence, teach me to plumb the depths of your love as you reveal
yourself more fully to me. Open my heart to you as your word continually gains
access into my life.

Remember that you were a slave in Egypt and the Lord your God redeemed you from there; therefore I command you to do this. DEUT 24:18

Remember the Alien, the Orphan, and the Widow

LEVITICUS 19:9-18 ⁹*When you reap the harvest of your land, you shall not reap to the very edges of your field, or gather the gleanings of your harvest. ¹⁰You shall not strip your vineyard bare, or gather the fallen grapes of your vineyard; you shall leave them for the poor and the alien: I am the Lord your God.*

¹¹You shall not steal; you shall not deal falsely; and you shall not lie to one another. ¹²And you shall not swear falsely by my name, profaning the name of your God: I am the Lord.

¹³You shall not defraud your neighbor; you shall not steal; and you shall not keep for yourself the wages of a laborer until morning. ¹⁴You shall not revile the deaf or put a stumbling block before the blind; you shall fear your God: I am the Lord.

¹⁵You shall not render an unjust judgment; you shall not be partial to the poor or defer to the great: with justice you shall judge your neighbor. ¹⁶You shall not go around as a slanderer among your people, and you shall not profit by the blood of your neighbor: I am the Lord.

¹⁷You shall not hate in your heart anyone of your kin; you shall reprove your neighbor, or you will incur guilt yourself. ¹⁸You shall not take vengeance or bear a grudge against any of your people, but you shall love your neighbor as yourself: I am the Lord.

DEUTERONOMY 24:17-22   [17]*You shall not deprive a resident alien or an orphan of justice; you shall not take a widow's garment in pledge.* [18]*Remember that you were a slave in Egypt and the Lord your God redeemed you from there; therefore I command you to do this.*

[19]*When you reap your harvest in your field and forget a sheaf in the field, you shall not go back to get it; it shall be left for the alien, the orphan, and the widow, so that the Lord your God may bless you in all your undertakings.* [20]*When you beat your olive trees, do not strip what is left; it shall be for the alien, the orphan, and the widow.*

[21]*When you gather the grapes of your vineyard, do not glean what is left; it shall be for the alien, the orphan, and the widow.* [22]*Remember that you were a slave in the land of Egypt; therefore I am commanding you to do this.*

Certain sections of the Torah of Israel contain social regulations for God's people. Since God has entered a covenant relationship with them, the people must live in a way that respects this relationship with the living God. The section of legislation in the Book of Leviticus is shown to have an integral relationship with the very name and nature of God. After each section of legislation, the name of God is inserted: "I am the Lord your God" or "I am the Lord." In Hebrew, "the Lord" is *YHWH*, the name of God revealed to Moses. This inclusion of God's name throughout the social regulations of the people indicates the essential connection between who God is and the kind of life God's people are to live. Because God is holy, God's people must express holiness in their daily lives; because God is just, Israel ought to live in a way that expresses justice to others; because God is merciful, the people must express mercy in their relationship with others.

This relationship between the name of God and social legislation parallels the preamble of the Ten Commandments: "I am the Lord your God, who brought you out of the land of Egypt, out of the house of slavery; you shall have no gods before me" (Exod 20:2; Deut 5:6). This not only indicates that these social laws reflect the very nature of God, but that they originate in the moral authority of the God who entered into covenant with Israel on Mount Sinai. These laws regulating the people's behavior toward one another are similar in their status to the Ten Commandments. Obedience to God's commands must include more than personal devotion to God; it requires that loyalty to God be expressed in deeds of justice and mercy. And this behavior toward others is not simply the necessary consequence of worshiping God, but it is the fundamental prerequisite that establishes the people as God's own.

The list of social legislation in Leviticus 19 uses multiple terms to describe those for whom God's people are obliged to care: "the poor," "the alien," "your neighbor," "laborer," "the deaf," "the blind," and "your kin." This inclusive list clearly indicates that God's people are not only obliged to show mercy to their neighbor within their own social status, but also and particularly the disabled and disadvantaged persons pushed to the edges of society. They include those persons whom the community may be tempted to ignore, perhaps even abuse, for economic or social gain. The final command, "you shall love your neighbor as yourself," is often isolated from its context, especially because it was chosen by Jesus as one of the two great commandments. But in its context, the full force of this regulation can be understood. The term "neighbor" includes all of the categories of disadvantaged people mentioned above, and the term "love" means "you shall not hate in your heart" and "you shall not take vengeance or bear a grudge." The merciful love required of God's people includes both attitude and action; it demands not only feeling love but also acting in ways that translate love into concrete deeds of mercy and compassion.

This social regulation included in both Leviticus and Deuteronomy includes a special concern for "the poor and the alien" and "the widow and the orphan." In order to render merciful care for the powerless and those in economic need, several laws require that some produce from the harvest of the field, the olive trees, and the vineyard be given to them. First, the ripe crops around the edges of the fields must not be harvested, but they should be left for those in need. Second, whenever stalks of grain fall to the ground when reaping, these "gleanings" must be left for the poor, the alien, the orphan, and the widow. Third, after the olive trees are beaten so that the olives fall to the ground to be collected, the tree must not then be stripped bare of the remaining olives. These must be left for the needy. And finally, any grape clusters not fully ripe at the harvest must be left to ripen and be collected later by those in need. Likewise, whatever grapes fall to the ground during the picking must remain there until they are collected by the needy and the powerless of the land.

Reflection and Discussion

- Why does the social legislation in the Torah demonstrate a particular concern for the poor, the alien, the orphan, and the widow? How careful am I to help meet their needs?

- The social precepts toward the poor, the immigrant, and the powerless are stated in terms of obligations, not voluntary charity. In what ways does this challenge our modern ideas of religious almsgiving?

- How can I translate Israel's obligations concerning the harvesting of grain, olives, and grapes to my own career, family, and budget?

Prayer

Lord God, because you are merciful and have extended compassion toward me, you desire that I extend mercy to those around me. Help me to see the connections between my personal devotion to you and the merciful care that I must demonstrate to people in need.

Know therefore that the Lord your God is God, the faithful God who maintains covenant loyalty with those who love him and keep his commandments, to a thousand generations. DEUT 7:9

God Chose You in Mercy

DEUTERONOMY 4:27-31 *²⁷The Lord will scatter you among the peoples; only a few of you will be left among the nations where the Lord will lead you. ²⁸There you will serve other gods made by human hands, objects of wood and stone that neither see, nor hear, nor eat, nor smell. ²⁹From there you will seek the Lord your God, and you will find him if you search after him with all your heart and soul. ³⁰In your distress, when all these things have happened to you in time to come, you will return to the Lord your God and heed him. ³¹Because the Lord your God is a merciful God, he will neither abandon you nor destroy you; he will not forget the covenant with your ancestors that he swore to them.*

DEUTERONOMY 7:6-13 *⁶For you are a people holy to the Lord your God; the Lord your God has chosen you out of all the peoples on earth to be his people, his treasured possession.*

⁷It was not because you were more numerous than any other people that the Lord set his heart on you and chose you—for you were the fewest of all peoples. ⁸It was because the Lord loved you and kept the oath that he swore to your ancestors, that the Lord has brought you out with a mighty hand, and redeemed you from the house of slavery, from the hand of Pharaoh king of Egypt. ⁹Know therefore that the Lord your God is God, the faithful God who maintains covenant loyalty with those who love him and keep his commandments, to a thousand generations, ¹⁰and who repays in their own person those who reject him. He does not delay but repays in their own person those who reject him. [11]Therefore, observe diligently the commandment—the statutes, and the ordinances—that I am commanding you today.

[12]If you heed these ordinances, by diligently observing them, the Lord your God will maintain with you the covenant loyalty that he swore to your ancestors; [13]he will love you, bless you, and multiply you; he will bless the fruit of your womb and the fruit of your ground, your grain and your wine and your oil, the increase of your cattle and the issue of your flock, in the land that he swore to your ancestors to give you.

The setting for the Book of Deuteronomy is the land of Moab where Moses addresses the people of Israel before his death. Moses looks backward to recount their years in the desert and the covenant made by God with the Israelites. He also looks forward, emphasizing the challenges of Israel's future in the land and the responsibilities of God's people to maintain the covenant. In these sections, Moses speaks about both the past and the future of the Israelites, why God selected them and their resultant obligations before God.

Moses states simply that God chose the Israelites out of all the peoples of the earth to be "his treasured possession" (7:6). They exist in a holy relationship with God in order to dedicate themselves to God's service, manifesting to the world what it means to live in covenant with God. Yet the knowledge of God's people that they possess this unique place in God's eyes creates the danger that they may presume that they have earned this gift or that they deserve this divine favor. So Moses makes it clear that the Israelites possess no attractive features or special attributes that would cause God to choose them out of all the peoples of the earth. In fact, quite the contrary.

The reason, then, for God's choice? Moses explains: "It was because the Lord loved you and kept the oath that he swore to your ancestors" (7:8). The only reason is God's love, a divine love that is faithful, steadfast, and loyal. This love of God is unconditional, not based on any merit or worthiness of the recipient, which is why we can speak of God's election of the Israelites as an act of divine grace and mercy.

This loving choice of God results in significant obligations for Israel's future life in the land. The text indicates a clear parallel between the attributes of God and those of God's people. God's loving choice of Israel must be reflected in Israel's response to God. The faithful God who keeps covenant expects Israel to honor the stipulations of the covenant as well. The God who loves Israel expects the people to love wholeheartedly in return. The loving God who extends mercy to Israel expects them to extend mercy to others, especially to those who are unworthy and undeserving.

Moses also looks into the distant future when God's people will be conquered by their enemies, deported to other nations, and scattered widely among other peoples until only a few of them are left (4:27). Because Israel will worship foreign gods and trample upon the statutes of the covenant, God's judgment will fall upon the people and the promises of the covenant will be reversed. Yet Moses assures them that no time will be too distant and no place too far away for Israel to come back to God. Beyond human sin and God's judgment, there is always confident hope.

The Israelites had learned early, when they sinned by creating the golden calf, that their survival depended not on their ability to keep the covenant but on God's merciful forgiveness and faithful love. The only condition for the restoration of God's people is repentance. Israel will "seek," "find," and "return" to the Lord. The basis of their hope, yesterday, today, and always, is the name and nature of God: "Because the Lord your God is a merciful God" (4:31).

Reflection and Discussion

- Why did God choose the Israelites out of all the peoples of the earth? What does God's choice mean for Israel's future?

- What difference does it make in children's lives to know that they are treasured by their parents? What difference does it make in my life to know that I am God's "treasured possession"?

- Why is it necessary to be loved before being able to love? How does being loved by God unconditionally enable me to love God and other people?

- What hope does this text about God's people offer to me? What is the source of my hope?

Prayer

Faithful God, thank you for loving me and choosing me as your treasured possession. Give me the desire to always return to you and to trust in your merciful forgiveness and faithful love.

The Lord set his heart in love on your ancestors alone
and chose you, their descendants after them,
out of all the peoples, as it is today. DEUT 10:15

What the Lord Requires of You

DEUTERONOMY 10:12-22 *¹²So now, O Israel, what does the Lord your God require of you? Only to fear the Lord your God, to walk in all his ways, to love him, to serve the Lord your God with all your heart and with all your soul, ¹³and to keep the commandments of the Lord your God and his decrees that I am commanding you today, for your own well-being. ¹⁴Although heaven and the heaven of heavens belong to the Lord your God, the earth with all that is in it, ¹⁵yet the Lord set his heart in love on your ancestors alone and chose you, their descendants after them, out of all the peoples, as it is today. ¹⁶Circumcise, then, the foreskin of your heart, and do not be stubborn any longer. ¹⁷For the Lord your God is God of gods and Lord of lords, the great God, mighty and awesome, who is not partial and takes no bribe, ¹⁸who executes justice for the orphan and the widow, and who loves the strangers, providing them food and clothing. ¹⁹You shall also love the stranger, for you were strangers in the land of Egypt. ²⁰You shall fear the Lord your God; him alone you shall worship; to him you shall hold fast, and by his name you shall swear. ²¹He is your praise; he is your God, who has done for you these great and awesome things that your own eyes have seen. ²²Your ancestors went down to Egypt seventy persons; and now the Lord your God has made you as numerous as the stars in heaven.*

I n light of all that God has mercifully given to you, "What does the Lord require of you?" The response to this question forms a kind of digest of the Torah, showing that God's claim upon the people of the covenant is not obscure or complex. The text sums up the essence of what God asks of the Israelites in five memorable phrases: to fear the Lord, to walk in God's ways, to love the Lord, to serve him, and to keep the commandments. This is what it means to be in covenant, to live in relationship with God. And these five acts are all done, as Moses says, "for your own well-being" (verse 13). The Torah and its stipulations are not God's arbitrary imposition; rather, they are a gift of God's mercy for the benefit of God's people.

The text then highlights the vastness of God and the particularity of God's love. There is absolutely nothing in creation that does not belong to God, yet the Lord has chosen to focus on the Israelites out of all the peoples of the earth (verses 14-15). The people's response, then, must be to open their hearts to God and to follow in the way of the Lord. The text uses the image of circumcision, the physical sign of the covenant, metaphorically. The inner commitment of the heart lives out the meaning of the physical mark in the flesh (verse 16). God's choice of Israel, then, is not so much a privilege as a tremendous responsibility.

Again, the text draws attention to God's greatness and the lowliness of those for whom God is concerned. Even though God is "mighty and awesome," the universal Lord over all other spiritual realities, this almighty God focuses his concern on the orphans, the widows, and the strangers (verses 17-18). This is the God of mercy. The divine compassion is for the poor and the powerless, the weak and the vulnerable.

In ancient texts from other cultures, the beneficiaries of the power exercised by the national gods are the royal family and others who are wealthy and powerful. In contrast, Israel's faith was countercultural. The fundamental character of God in the Bible is mercy. And as we have seen in other texts, this quality of mercy pervades the social legislations of the Torah and explicitly shapes the behavior that God desires from his people. Since God "loves the strangers"—the aliens, the immigrants, the refugees—then, the text commands, "You shall also love the stranger" (verse 19).

The Torah contains only a few phrases in which God's people are commanded to love. Twice the Israelites are commanded, "You shall love the

Lord your God" (Deut 6:5; 11:1). Once they are commanded, "You shall love your neighbor" (Lev 19:18). And in the Book of Leviticus and here in this text, they are commanded, "You shall love the alien/stranger" (Lev 19:34; Deut 10:19). In each command, what God requires of Israel is what God has first demonstrated to them. Only because God has first loved them could the Israelites love God and also love those in their midst who are in need.

The Israelites had learned about God's disposition toward the strangers when they themselves were "strangers in the land of Egypt" (verse 19). God has shown merciful love for the aliens living in a foreign land; so now these refugees from Egypt must show mercy to the aliens in their own land. To walk in God's ways, to love the Lord, to serve him, and to keep the commandments, Israel must "love the stranger." Throughout the Bible, social ethics involves the imitation of God's ways.

The Book of Deuteronomy is preparing God's people for their life in the land from generation to generation, and for this reason, God commands Israel not only to love God and love their neighbor, but to "love the stranger." God knows that love of the immigrants and refugees is the first characteristic of a society to dissolve in times of economic scarcity and social conflict. The aliens and strangers are the first to experience bigotry and scapegoating. The Israelites suffered intolerant racism and were made slaves in Egypt. Now they must make certain that they follow God's example and maintain mercy and focused compassion for the strangers and dispossessed in their midst.

Reflection and Discussion

- Moses tells the people that obeying the commandments is for their own well-being. In what ways do I experience following God's law as being for my own good?

- In what ways does this text demonstrate that mercy is God's fundamental character?

- Why does God specifically command the Israelites to love the stranger? What occasions have I had to obey this command?

- In what particular ways can I better live up to God's standard of mercy in my dealings with others?

Prayer

Merciful God, you care for your people in need and teach them to love the strangers and aliens in their midst. Show me how to love and serve you, to walk in your ways, and to keep your commandments by loving those whom you love.

"The Creator of the world, who shaped the beginning of humankind and devised the origin of all things, will in his mercy give life and breath back to you again." 2 MACC 7:23

The Ultimate Gift
of Divine Mercy

2 MACCABEES 7:20-29 *²⁰The mother was especially admirable and worthy of honorable memory. Although she saw her seven sons perish within a single day, she bore it with good courage because of her hope in the Lord. ²¹She encouraged each of them in the language of their ancestors. Filled with a noble spirit, she reinforced her woman's reasoning with a man's courage, and said to them,²²"I do not know how you came into being in my womb. It was not I who gave you life and breath, nor I who set in order the elements within each of you. ²³Therefore the Creator of the world, who shaped the beginning of humankind and devised the origin of all things, will in his mercy give life and breath back to you again, since you now forget yourselves for the sake of his laws."*

²⁴Antiochus felt that he was being treated with contempt, and he was suspicious of her reproachful tone. The youngest brother being still alive, Antiochus not only appealed to him in words, but promised with oaths that he would make him rich and enviable if he would turn from the ways of his ancestors, and that he would take him for his Friend and entrust him with public affairs. ²⁵Since the young man would not listen to him at all, the king called the mother to him and urged her to advise the youth to save himself. ²⁶After much urging on his part, she undertook to persuade her son. ²⁷But, leaning close to him, she spoke in their native language as follows, deriding the cruel tyrant: "My son, have pity on me. I carried you nine *months in my womb, and nursed you for three years, and have reared you and brought you up to this point in your life, and have taken care of you. *[28]*I beg you, my child, to look at the heaven and the earth and see everything that is in them, and recognize that God did not make them out of things that existed. And in the same way the human race came into being. *[29]*Do not fear this butcher, but prove worthy of your brothers. Accept death, so that in God's mercy I may get you back again along with your brothers."*

Again and again, the Bible describes the mercy and faithfulness of God in difficult and humanly hopeless situations. This account of a mother and her seven sons takes place in a time of persecution near the end of the Old Testament period, around 168 BC. The Greek ruler Antiochus Epiphanes tried to force the Jews to give up the practices of their faith and adopt the ways of the Greek culture. The writer recounts the story of seven brothers who were arrested along with their mother. When they refused to eat pork as the king demanded, he subjected the brothers to torture, one by one, in their mother's presence. Each of them remained faithful to God's law, despite their terrible suffering and death.

The valiant mother encouraged her sons to remain strong and to trust in God. As she addresses them, she marvels at the ways that God has created each of her sons in her womb, giving them life and breath (verse 22). She proclaims that God, who has created the world and humankind, will give life and breath back to them again (verse 23). She trusts that the merciful God who created each one of her sons in her own womb will perform a mighty act of new creation in which these martyrs will be given new bodies and a new breath of God.

Our individual creation by God gives us an eternal perspective for looking at our lives. We are completely in God's hands. The God who made us and gave us life will not allow us to perish forever. This is a hope that gives freedom. We can remain in hope of eternal life even in a fearful death or martyrdom. Eternal life is God's ultimate gift of mercy.

After the martyrdom of six of the brothers, Antiochus promises wealth and honor to the seventh and urges the mother to advise him to save himself. But the wise and courageous mother invites her son to look to the heavens and the earth and recognize their Creator. She trusts that the God who made her sons and gave them life will raise them again to life: "Accept death, so that in God's mercy I may get you back again along with your brothers" (verse 29).

The resurrection of the dead will take place at the last judgment, as believed by Jews in this period and later specified by Jesus in his teachings. In Jesus' rising from the dead, this hope was definitively sealed for the first Christians. In the fullness of time the dead will be raised to life, a time that believers can look forward to with joyful hope. This last judgment will manifest God's mercy as well as divine justice.

Reflection and Discussion

- In what way does the courageous love of the mother for her children offer a unique insight into the mercy of God?

- Compare your hope with that of the mother and her seven sons. What gives you confidence in God's unending mercy?

Prayer

Creator and Redeemer, in mercy you created the world and in mercy you have saved it. Help me to realize that my existence is in your hands and to understand my whole life in terms of your mercy.

SUGGESTIONS FOR GROUP SESSION 2

1. If there are newcomers who were not present for the first group session, introduce them now.

2. You may want to pray this prayer as a group:
   Lord God, you are merciful, compassionate, forgiving, and filled with committed love for us. Help us to realize that you created and redeemed the world in mercy and that our lives are totally dependent on you. As we study these ancient Scriptures, open our hearts to your word as you reveal yourself more fully and teach us how to extend mercy to those around us. Help us to see the connections between our personal devotion to you and the merciful compassion that we must demonstrate to the strangers and aliens in our midst.

3. Ask one or more of the following questions:
   - What was your biggest challenge in Bible study over this past week?
   - What did you learn about yourself this week?

4. Discuss lessons 1 through 6 together. Assuming that group members have read the Scripture and commentary during the week, there is no need to read it aloud. As you review each lesson, you might want to briefly summarize the Scripture passages of each lesson and ask the group what stands out most clearly from the commentary.

5. Choose one or more of the questions for reflection and discussion from each lesson to talk over as a group. You may want to ask group members which question was most helpful to them as you review each lesson.

6. Keep the discussion moving, but don't rush the discussion in order to complete more questions. Allow time for the questions that provoke the most discussion.

7. Instruct group members to complete lessons 7 through 12 on their own during the six days before the next group meeting. They should write out their own answers to the questions as preparation for next week's group discussion.

8. Conclude by praying aloud together the prayer at the end of lesson 6, or any other prayer you choose.

I will take you for my wife forever; I will take you for my wife in righteousness and in justice, in steadfast love, and in mercy.

HOS 2:19

God Pursues His Beloved

HOSEA 2:14-23

¹⁴*Therefore, I will now persuade her,*
   and bring her into the wilderness,
   and speak tenderly to her.
¹⁵*From there I will give her her vineyards,*
   and make the Valley of Achor a door of hope.
There she shall respond as in the days of her youth,
   as at the time when she came out of the land of Egypt.

¹⁶*On that day, says the Lord, you will call me, "My husband," and no longer will you call me, "My Baal."* ¹⁷*For I will remove the names of the Baals from her mouth, and they shall be mentioned by name no more.* ¹⁸*I will make for you a covenant on that day with the wild animals, the birds of the air, and the creeping things of the ground; and I will abolish the bow, the sword, and war from the land; and I will make you lie down in safety.* ¹⁹*And I will take you for my wife forever; I will take you for my wife in righteousness and in justice, in steadfast love, and in mercy.* ²⁰*I will take you for my wife in faithfulness; and you shall know the Lord.*

²¹*On that day I will answer, says the Lord,*
   I will answer the heavens
   and they shall answer the earth;
²²*and the earth shall answer the grain, the wine, and the oil,*
   and they shall answer Jezreel;

23and I will sow him for myself in the land.
And I will have pity on Lo-ruhamah,
and I will say to Lo-ammi, "You are my people";
and he shall say, "You are my God."

N o prophet of the Bible expresses God's merciful love more wonderfully than Hosea. The prophet offers the image of a husband and wife in marriage to express the relationship of God to his people. Paul will later use a similar image for the relationship of Christ and his church. Because there is no human experience more intimate than marriage, no experience is more suitable for conveying the relationship that God desires to have with us.

Hosea's own marriage was far from ideal, yet he uses his own experiences to provide an analogy for God's marriage with his people. Even though Israel had been unfaithful to God in order to pursue the Baals, the fertility gods of the surrounding cultures, God refuses to cast her aside or give up on her. Instead, God continues to pursue Israel, as a lover pursues his beloved. The penalties she experiences for her infidelity are not acts of vengeance, but are meant to chasten the beloved and win her back.

God determines that he will bring Israel out into the wilderness as he did at the beginning of their relationship after Israel was freed from the bonds of Egypt (verses 14-15). God will, in a sense, begin their relationship anew. There, in the wilderness, where no Baal can come between them, God will "speak tenderly" to her and woo the heart of his bride back to himself. As God leads Israel back toward her land, the Valley of Achor, which means literally "valley of trouble," will become for Israel a "door of hope," leading her into a new relationship with God and a new life.

God's promises for Israel's future assure her of security. Sin not only disrupts human relationships but also human bonds with the natural world, so God assured Israel of a new harmony with the creatures of the earth and the abolition of weapons of war from the land (verse 18). Then, having assured Israel of her safety and established a bond of trust, God will enter into a formal betrothal with his beloved people, a faithful and lasting marital covenant (verse 19). The Lord pledges to bestow upon his wife the gifts of righteousness, justice, steadfast love, and mercy. These are the qualities that will characterize their life together. Then, Israel will truly "know the Lord," a key expression in the writings of Hosea to describe the intimate relationship and mutual devotion between God and his people (verse 20).

The establishment of this new and everlasting marital covenant is anticipated for the coming age of God's kingdom. In this messianic age of the new covenant, God's people will lack for nothing. The Lord will call the heavens to bring forth rain, and the earth will give forth grain, grapes, and olives, crying out with joy, "Jezreel," that is, "God sows" (verse 22). Israel will respond to God with trust and surrender. This era of the new covenant is the result of God's action, a work that Israel has done nothing to earn or deserve. It is God's great act of mercy toward his people, gathering up all the promises of God in the old covenant and bringing them to fulfillment.

Reflection and Discussion

- Why is marriage a particularly effective image to express God's mercy?

- In what ways do I experience God's spousal mercy in my own life?

- Why does God bring Israel out into the wilderness to begin their relationship anew?

- How have I experienced a "valley of trouble" becoming a "door of hope" leading me to a fuller life?

- In light of these words of Hosea, why is it significant that Jesus begins his ministry in the wilderness? In what ways is his coming a time of mercy for God's people?

Prayer

Divine Lover, your affection for me and your desire for me to return your love are greater than I can imagine. Although I often stray from your love, teach me how great is your mercy toward me.

He will again have compassion upon us; he will tread our iniquities under foot. You will cast all our sins into the depths of the sea. MIC 7:19

God Delights in Showing Mercy

MICAH 6:6-8

⁶"With what shall I come before the Lord,
  and bow myself before God on high?
Shall I come before him with burnt offerings,
  with calves a year old?
⁷Will the Lord be pleased with thousands of rams,
  with ten thousands of rivers of oil?
Shall I give my firstborn for my transgression,
  the fruit of my body for the sin of my soul?"
⁸He has told you, O mortal, what is good;
  and what does the Lord require of you
but to do justice, and to love kindness,
  and to walk humbly with your God?

MICAH 7:18-20

¹⁸Who is a God like you, pardoning iniquity
  and passing over the transgression
  of the remnant of your possession?
He does not retain his anger forever,

because he delights in showing clemency.
¹⁹He will again have compassion upon us;
  he will tread our iniquities under foot.
You will cast all our sins
  into the depths of the sea.
²⁰You will show faithfulness to Jacob
  and unswerving loyalty to Abraham,
as you have sworn to our ancestors
  from the days of old.

What does God want from me? "With what shall I come before the Lord?" the speaker asks in an increasingly exasperated tone (6:6-7). Apparently the situation is desperate, and the speaker wants to know how on earth God's people can make things right with God. How about animal sacrifices, burned with a pleasing odor sent up to God? Maybe the Lord would prefer calves a year old, because calves increase in value from the time of their birth. Would thousands of rams, the size of Solomon's offering, please God? Or perhaps fine olive oil poured out in immeasurable abundance would be enough to satisfy the Lord. The step-by-step escalation continues as the speaker asks if God would want a child offered in sacrifice, the firstborn of one's body offered for sin. The sacrifice of children was often practiced by Israel's neighbors but was clearly forbidden in Israel's law and condemned by the prophets. What could possibly please God?

Since this text was proclaimed in Israel's public liturgy, perhaps the response was read by another voice (6:8). God's answer to such sarcastic questioning is simple. The questions were based on the false assumption that God wants some material substance from his people. But, in fact, God has already told them what is the divine will and what the Lord requires. God does not want any *thing* from them. Rather, God desires a way of living. In broad outline, the three statements of God's will express the Torah and the prophets of Israel in a nutshell.

God's first requirement is that his people "do justice." The prophet has already preached against the failure to do justice: oppressing the powerless, exploiting workers, corrupting the courts. Doing justice means setting up a

society in which fairness and equity is practiced for people. God's second requirement is that the people "love kindness." This means practicing mercy, being faithful to the covenant obligations of treating others with mutual respect
and care. And the final requirement is that people "walk humbly" with God.
This implies living day by day in union with God's word, paying attention to
God's will, and not just following one's own desires. This daily, attentive walk
with God makes it possible to practice justice and mercy.

The prophetic Book of Micah concludes with a rhetorical question: "Who
is a God like you?" (7:18). And the implied answer, of course, is "There is no
God like you." The reason why God is incomparable with the gods of any other nation is because the Lord shows mercy. Then the book ends with a flurry
of seven ways that God has demonstrated divine mercy to Israel's ancestors
and continues to show mercy to this day.

First, God pardons iniquity. The phrase suggests that the Lord removes
sin by taking the guilt off his people. Second, God passes over their transgression. As God passed over the Israelites during the destruction in Egypt, so
God spares his people from their sin. Third, God "does not retain his anger."
Gratefully, the Lord's anger lasts only a moment and his mercy for a lifetime.
Fourth, God "delights in showing clemency." God's very nature is to have mercy and forgive. Fifth, God will have "compassion." This is the kind of merciful
love that parents have for their children. Sixth, God will "tread our iniquities
under foot." As enemies are trampled in warfare, the Lord will stamp out our
guilt. And seventh, God will "cast all our sins into the depths of the sea." The
Lord will pick up all our sins and hurl them into the sea, where they will be
completely removed from God's sight. Surely there is no God like our merciful Lord.

Reflection and Discussion

- Why are abundant sacrifices unable to please God?

- How is God unlike the gods of the peoples surrounding ancient Israel? What does this imply about the relationship of the Israelites with their God?

- What can I do better today in order to "walk humbly" with God?

- Consider the seven ways that God demonstrates divine mercy. How does this challenge my conception of the God of Israel?

Prayer

How great is your mercy, Lord our God! How wonderful is your desire to pardon me! Give me the grace to be compassionate as you are compassionate, to be forgiving as you are forgiving.

Let the wicked forsake their way, and the unrighteous
their thoughts; let them return to the Lord, that he may have
mercy on them, and to our God, for he will abundantly pardon.

ISA 55:7

God's Everlasting Compassion and Mercy

ISAIAH 54:4-10

4Do not fear, for you will not be ashamed;
  do not be discouraged, for you will not suffer disgrace;
for you will forget the shame of your youth,
  and the disgrace of your widowhood you will remember no more.
5For your Maker is your husband,
  the Lord of hosts is his name;
the Holy One of Israel is your Redeemer,
  the God of the whole earth he is called.
6For the Lord has called you
  like a wife forsaken and grieved in spirit,
like the wife of a man's youth when she is cast off,
  says your God.
7For a brief moment I abandoned you,
  but with great compassion I will gather you.
8In overflowing wrath for a moment
  I hid my face from you,
but with everlasting love I will have compassion on you,

says the Lord, your Redeemer.
⁹This is like the days of Noah to me:
　Just as I swore that the waters of Noah
　would never again go over the earth,
so I have sworn that I will not be angry with you
　and will not rebuke you.
¹⁰For the mountains may depart
　and the hills be removed,
but my steadfast love shall not depart from you,
　and my covenant of peace shall not be removed,
　says the Lord, who has compassion on you.

ISAIAH 55:6-9

⁶Seek the Lord while he may be found,
　call upon him while he is near;
⁷let the wicked forsake their way,
　and the unrighteous their thoughts;
let them return to the Lord, that he may have mercy on them,
　and to our God, for he will abundantly pardon.
⁸For my thoughts are not your thoughts,
　nor are your ways my ways, says the Lord.
⁹For as the heavens are higher than the earth,
　so are my ways higher than your ways
　and my thoughts than your thoughts.

The prophet offers images of devastating disappointment to address the situation of God's people: childlessness, widowhood, disgrace, divorce, abandonment. Anyone who has suffered personal loss connects on a deeply personal level with the emotional pain in these passages. The historical setting of Isaiah's prophecy is the destruction of Jerusalem and the exile of God's people in Babylon. Israel is like a woman who feels that her troubles are due to her abandonment by her husband. She is "like a wife forsaken and grieved," like a wife "when she is cast off" (54:6).

But God now announces the end of Israel's humiliation. The Lord proclaims that God's people need not fear or be discouraged, for Israel will forget her shame and disgrace. How can she know this? Because the husband whose absence she laments is Israel's Maker, "the Holy One of Israel" and also "the God of the whole earth" (verse 5). Then God replies with assurances of mercy and love to Israel's complaint that the Lord has forsaken her. Like a good husband, the Lord does not blame the other or deny the real pain that their separation has caused. Rather, God contrasts the "brief moment" in which he "abandoned" Israel with the "great compassion" with which he will take her back (54:7). He distinguishes the "overflowing wrath" that lasted only "for a moment" and the "everlasting love" with which he will have compassion on his beloved (54:8). A more beautiful expression of mercy would be difficult to find in any literature.

Israel wants to know how she can be sure that God's wrath has been overcome by everlasting love. God must further reassure Israel by providing a guarantee that the catastrophe will not just continue to repeat itself. So the Lord recalls the story of Noah and the divine pledge never to destroy the earth again. Like God's pledge to Noah, God pledges that he will not remain angry with Israel nor will he rebuke her (54:9). The story of Noah becomes the basis for God's incredible promise: "For the mountains may depart and the hills be removed, but my steadfast love shall not depart from you, and my covenant of peace shall not be removed" (54:10). God's words are filled with passion and conviction. Not only is God a dependable and trustworthy husband to Israel; truly God has compassion on his people and guides their history in order to redeem them.

The words of the prophet recall a time of deep suffering for Israel. But in retrospect, even the disaster of Israel's exile became an aspect of God's mercy for his people. Because through the exile, the Israelites would be purified of their idolatry and injustices, thus becoming able once again to enter into an intimate relationship with the Lord. Likewise, we can understand even the painful adversity of our lives as an aspect of God's mercy toward us. For God cares for us with deep compassion and with an everlasting love.

Because of such inconceivable mercy, the prophet then urges the people to "seek the Lord" and to "call upon him" (55:6). He enjoins sinners to convert in thought and deed, returning to the Lord that he may "have mercy on them" and "abundantly pardon" them (55:7). Casting one's life into the arms of such a merciful God requires trust because God's thoughts and intentions are so unlike those of mortals (55:8). God's mercy stands above our logic of guilt and punishment. God is merciful without contradicting divine justice. God's mercy is faithful and so much higher than our own ways.

Reflection and Discussion

- Has hardship or disappointment ever tempted me to withdraw from my relationship with God? What emotions did I feel in that situation?

- How have I experienced God drawing me back to himself after a time of separation? How has God convinced me of his faithful love?

- What has persuaded me to believe that God's thoughts and ways are infinitely higher and greater than my own?

Prayer

Holy One of Israel, you are eternally faithful to your people, and your compassion is without limit. You use my painful experiences to draw me to yourself. Help me to trust in your mercy and to see your hand at work even in my adversity and failures.

But you, O Lord, are a God merciful and gracious, slow to anger and abounding in steadfast love and faithfulness. PS 86:15

Great Is Your Steadfast Love

PSALM 86:1-17

¹Incline your ear, O Lord, and answer me,
   for I am poor and needy.
²Preserve my life, for I am devoted to you;
   save your servant who trusts in you.
You are my God; ³be gracious to me, O Lord,
   for to you do I cry all day long.
⁴Gladden the soul of your servant,
   for to you, O Lord, I lift up my soul.
⁵For you, O Lord, are good and forgiving,
   abounding in steadfast love to all who call on you.
⁶Give ear, O Lord, to my prayer;
   listen to my cry of supplication.
⁷In the day of my trouble I call on you,
   for you will answer me.
⁸There is none like you among the gods, O Lord,
   nor are there any works like yours.
⁹All the nations you have made shall come
   and bow down before you, O Lord,
   and shall glorify your name.

^{10}*For you are great and do wondrous things;*
  you alone are God.
^{11}*Teach me your way, O Lord,*
  that I may walk in your truth;
  give me an undivided heart to revere your name.
^{12}*I give thanks to you, O Lord my God, with my whole heart,*
  and I will glorify your name forever.
^{13}*For great is your steadfast love toward me;*
  you have delivered my soul from the depths of Sheol.
^{14}*O God, the insolent rise up against me;*
  a band of ruffians seeks my life,
  and they do not set you before them.
^{15}*But you, O Lord, are a God merciful and gracious,*
  slow to anger and abounding in steadfast love and faithfulness.
^{16}*Turn to me and be gracious to me;*
  give your strength to your servant;
  save the child of your serving girl.
^{17}*Show me a sign of your favor,*
  so that those who hate me may see it and be put to shame,
  because you, Lord, have helped me and comforted me.

The psalms express God's mercy with poetic beauty. This psalm of lament, like the other laments in the psalter, doesn't conclude with complaint, anguish, and gloom. Rather, it gradually becomes a song of trust and gratitude. This is the reason that Jesus prayed Psalm 22 from the cross. Although it begins with desolation—"My God, why have you forsaken me?"—it moves toward expressions of hope and thanksgiving. Likewise, Psalm 86 opens with a distressed plea to God; it concludes with confidence in the Lord's mercy.

This psalm is composed of a variety of expressions found throughout Scripture. This reuse of traditional vocabulary and phrases creates a unique prayer to God offered in a time of need. It focuses on the character of God and on the identity of the one praying in relationship to God. The words are familiar but the plea is heartfelt, so the psalm can be prayed by anyone living within the covenant between God and his people.

The prayer begins with a long series of petitions to God: incline your ear and answer me, preserve my life, save your servant, be gracious to me, lift up my soul, give ear to my prayer, and listen to me (verses 1-6). Each plea is supported by a statement about the one who prays in relationship to God: for I am poor and needy, for I am devoted to you, for to you I cry, for to you I lift up my soul. The person praying denies all self-sufficiency and admits that life is totally dependent on God. Each petition is an expression of confidence that God will respond: "I call on you, for you will answer me" (verse 7). The familiar phrase, praising God as "good and forgiving, abounding in steadfast love," reaching back to the tradition of the exodus, describes a dependable God of unchanging character, tested through generations of believers.

The central section of the psalm is a prayer of praise, infinitely expanding the characteristics of God (verses 8-10). The personal God who hears and answers the prayers of each individual is also the universal and only God. God works with unlimited power and unrivaled authority. The Lord is the Creator of all the nations, and all people will, in due time, offer homage to God and glorify the divine name.

The final section of the prayer returns to petitions, pleading not only for deliverance in time of trouble, but also for a lifestyle and inner character that offers God praise and thanks. The psalmist prays for an understanding of God's ways and "an undivided heart" to give wholehearted thanks to God and to glorify God's name forever (verses 11-12). The prayer alternates between personal petitions (verses 14, 16) and words of praise for God from Israel's tradition (verses 13, 15). So the prayer is based both on the personal trust of an individual and on the ancient faith of the whole people of Israel.

The confidence of the individual praying the psalms is rooted in what Israel has known about God from the earliest times. The ancient liturgical confession found in Exodus 34:6 is inserted here as an expression of this ancient faith: "You, O Lord, are a God merciful and gracious, slow to anger and abounding in steadfast love and faithfulness" (verse 15). So the psalmist prays with confidence rooted in God's revelation of divine mercy and the faith of God's people who have experienced that mercy through the ages.

Reflection and Discussion

- What is the advantage for an individual when praying within a wide and deep tradition of faith?

- The psalmist describes many characteristics of God through this prayer. Which divine attribute might affect my relationship with God if I call upon it in prayer?

- What enables the psalmist to trust in God? What helps me to have confidence in God and to pray with expectancy?

Prayer

Lord my God, because you have been merciful and gracious, abounding in steadfast love and faithfulness to my ancestors, I can trust in you and pray with confidence. Teach me your ways that I may walk in your truth; give me an undivided heart to revere your name.

The Lord is merciful and gracious, slow to anger and abounding in steadfast love. PS 103:8

Our Creator's Mercy Is Everlasting

PSALM 103:1-18

¹*Bless the Lord, O my soul,*
  and all that is within me,
  bless his holy name.
²*Bless the Lord, O my soul,*
  and do not forget all his benefits—
³*who forgives all your iniquity,*
  who heals all your diseases,
⁴*who redeems your life from the Pit,*
  who crowns you with steadfast love and mercy,
⁵*who satisfies you with good as long as you live*
  so that your youth is renewed like the eagle's.
⁶*The Lord works vindication*
  and justice for all who are oppressed.
⁷*He made known his ways to Moses,*
  his acts to the people of Israel.
⁸*The Lord is merciful and gracious,*
  slow to anger and abounding in steadfast love.
⁹*He will not always accuse,*
  nor will he keep his anger forever.

^{10}He does not deal with us according to our sins,
  nor repay us according to our iniquities.
^{11}For as the heavens are high above the earth,
  so great is his steadfast love toward those who fear him;
^{12}as far as the east is from the west,
  so far he removes our transgressions from us.
^{13}As a father has compassion for his children,
  so the Lord has compassion for those who fear him.
^{14}For he knows how we were made;
  he remembers that we are dust.
^{15}As for mortals, their days are like grass;
  they flourish like a flower of the field;
^{16}for the wind passes over it, and it is gone,
  and its place knows it no more.
^{17}But the steadfast love of the Lord is from everlasting to everlasting
  on those who fear him,
  and his righteousness to children's children,
^{18}to those who keep his covenant
  and remember to do his commandments.

The psalm provides a prayer of praise for God's mercy. It recites in a concentrated way what Israel has learned about the ways of God. The prayer gives expression to the gratitude of all sinners that the Lord is a God of mercy. The words of the psalm have been the means of remembering in age after age that God is gracious and forgiving, abounding in mercy and steadfast love.

The relationship of the Lord to sinners is a theme running throughout the psalm. The verses echo the account of Israel's sin with the golden calf, remembering that God "made known his ways to Moses, his acts to the people of Israel" (verse 7). Most prominent is the ancient confession of God's mercy: "The Lord is merciful and gracious, slow to anger and abounding in steadfast love" (verse 8).

The psalm includes the three words of the Old Testament for human offenses, translated here as "iniquity" (verse 3), "sins" (verse 10), and "transgressions" (verse 12). The verses do not ignore the reality of God's wrath but focus on its delay, its brevity, and its sparing application. God is "slow to anger" (verse 8); God will not keep his anger forever (verse 9); and God will "not deal with us according to our sins nor repay us according to our iniquities" (verse 10). As Israel's ancient confession of Exodus states, God keeps "steadfast love for the thousandth generation, forgiving iniquity and transgression and sin" (Exod 34:7).

The psalmist offers three comparisons to emphasize the extent of God's mercy. The first speaks of vertical spaciousness: "As the heavens are high above the earth, so great is his steadfast love toward those who fear him" (verse 11). The second conveys horizontal spaciousness: "As far as the east is from the west, so far he removes our transgressions from us" (verse 12). And the third expresses a relationship comparison: "As a father has compassion for his children, so the Lord has compassion for those who fear him" (verse 13).

The entire psalm concerns the importance of remembering. God's people are told to remind themselves of all God has done for them: "Do not forget all his benefits" (verse 2). This remembering also concerns God's memory, which goes back to the very beginning of creation: "For he knows how we were made; he remembers that we are dust" (verse 14). God remembers the frailty and brevity of human existence, for mortals are like the fleeting life of grass, like the wilting flower (verse 15). For this reason, God's people must remember their relationship with God and keep the commandments of the covenant (verse 18). For them, God's mercy is "from everlasting to everlasting," having no beginning or end (verse 17). The psalm is a wonderful way to remember, for there is nothing more important for us sinners than to remember always the goodness of God's mercy.

Reflection and Discussion

- What are some of the words and phrases of this psalm that express God's mercy?

- How does this psalm convince me that God does not deal with me in the way that my sins deserve?

- The psalm is a marvelous way to remember the everlasting mercy of God. What do I particularly want to remember about what God has done for me?

- The psalm contrasts the brevity of our human lives (verses 14-16) with the height, breadth, and intensity of God's mercy (verses 11-13). How does meditating on this reality deepen my faith in God?

Prayer

Compassionate Father, your mercy is without beginning or end for those in covenant with you. May I always remember your steadfast love and never forget the forgiveness and many blessings you have given me.

O give thanks to the God of gods, for his steadfast love
endures forever. O give thanks to the Lord of lords,
for his steadfast love endures forever. PS 136:2-3

Litany of God's Mercy

PSALM 136:1-16, 23-26

¹*O give thanks to the Lord, for he is good,*
for his steadfast love endures forever.
²*O give thanks to the God of gods,*
for his steadfast love endures forever.
³*O give thanks to the Lord of lords,*
for his steadfast love endures forever;
⁴*who alone does great wonders,*
for his steadfast love endures forever;
⁵*who by understanding made the heavens,*
for his steadfast love endures forever;
⁶*who spread out the earth on the waters,*
for his steadfast love endures forever;
⁷*who made the great lights,*
for his steadfast love endures forever;
⁸*the sun to rule over the day,*
for his steadfast love endures forever;
⁹*the moon and stars to rule over the night,*
for his steadfast love endures forever;
¹⁰*who struck Egypt through their firstborn,*
for his steadfast love endures forever;

¹¹*and brought Israel out from among them,*
  for his steadfast love endures forever;
¹²*with a strong hand and an outstretched arm,*
  for his steadfast love endures forever;
¹³*who divided the Red Sea in two,*
  for his steadfast love endures forever;
¹⁴*and made Israel pass through the midst of it,*
  for his steadfast love endures forever;
¹⁵*but overthrew Pharaoh and his army in the Red Sea,*
  for his steadfast love endures forever;
¹⁶*who led his people through the wilderness,*
  for his steadfast love endures forever.

²³*It is he who remembered us in our low estate,*
  for his steadfast love endures forever;
²⁴*and rescued us from our foes,*
  for his steadfast love endures forever;
²⁵*who gives food to all flesh,*
  for his steadfast love endures forever.
²⁶*O give thanks to the God of heaven,*
  for his steadfast love endures forever.

This psalm is a song of thanksgiving for God's mercy. It begins and ends with an exhortation to give thanks to God. Each verse contains the refrain, "For his steadfast love endures forever," which is often translated as "For his mercy endures forever." The psalm is in the form of a litany, meant to be prayed by a leader chanting the first half of each verse and the congregation responding with the refrain.

For the Israelites, God's mercy and faithful love was manifested by the works of the Lord, and they gave thanks to God by acknowledging these divine deeds. The opening verse is a phrase from Israel's liturgical acclamations: "O give thanks to the Lord, for he is good, for his steadfast love endures forever." The same formula introduces Psalms 106, 107, and 118, and it may also be found in other parts of Israel's Scriptures. This call to worship is a plural imperative, meaning it was most probably addressed to a worshiping congregation.

The first three verses are an extended invitation to give thanks to God, calling on the "God of gods" and the "Lord of lords" (verses 1-3). The next verse expresses what will be praised throughout: the "great wonders" done by God alone (verse 4). The first list of wonders focuses on God's creation of the universe (verses 4-9). Then the litany turns to the events of the exodus, praising God for freeing the people from slavery during the time of Moses (verses 10-16).

The final verses of the psalm change the structure in order to emphasize that God's people today share in the great deeds of the past. God has "remembered us in our low estate" and "rescued us from our foes" (verses 23-24), explicitly including those present within the history of God's wonderful deeds. Then the thanksgiving becomes universal as God is praised as the one "who gives food to all flesh" (verse 25).

As the psalm draws upon God's deeds in the tradition of Israel, its purpose is to consider how the deeds of the past impinge on the present, enabling those praying to realize that God's continuing work is the result of divine constancy throughout the ages. In addition, this same faithfulness of God assures those praying that their future will be marked by God's steadfast love. The psalm expresses the identity of the Lord whose merciful love embraces all time—past, present, and future.

The last verse returns to the invitation to give thanks to God, as in the opening verses. God is given another title: "the God of heaven." Along with the names of God and the other divine titles of the opening verses, this title emphasizes that the purpose of the psalm is not so much to thank the Lord for doing all these things, but rather to thank the one whose divine nature and identity is made known in and through these many wonders. The litany of God's merciful deeds makes known the person of God. The name and the nature of God receives its reality and actuality as God is connected with the world and the story of Israel. And the world and the story of Israel become worthy of praise and thanksgiving as they are understood as the marvelous works of the Lord.

The story contained in Israel's tradition is always being made contemporary by the congregation. If we were to compose a litany of thanksgiving to

God based on this psalm, we would extend the list of God's deeds to what God has done for us in Jesus Christ. And then we could personalize the litany by mentioning what the Lord has done for us in our own individual lives. The response for all of these, of course, would be the same: For his faithful love endures forever. God's mercy is everlasting.

Reflection and Discussion

- Why is it vitally important to verbally and explicitly give thanks to God? Why is it important to do the same for people in our lives?

- The psalm gives thanks to God for his wondrous deeds, from the creation of the world to the food we eat (verse 25)? How can I transform my ordinary meals into grateful encounters with God?

- What are some of the great deeds of God in my life that I could list in this litany of thanksgiving?

Prayer

O give thanks to the God of heaven, for his mercy endures forever. Who gave me life through my mother's womb, for his mercy endures forever. Who called me to new life through my baptism into Jesus Christ, for his mercy endures forever…

SUGGESTIONS FOR FACILITATORS, GROUP SESSION 3

1. Welcome group members and ask if there are any announcements anyone would like to make.

2. You may want to pray this prayer as a group:
   Lord God, how great is your mercy and how wonderful is your desire to forgive us. May we never forget your faithfulness and always remember your steadfast love for us. As the divine lover of your people, your tender affection invites us to return to you when we stray. As our compassionate parent, your desire that we return your love is greater than we can imagine. As we gather to study your word in the Bible, help us encourage one another and guide us with your Holy Spirit of truth. Inspire new hope within us, assure us of your presence, and guide us in your will.

3. Ask one or more of the following questions:
   - Which message of Scripture this week speaks most powerfully to you?
   - What is the most important lesson you learned through your study this week?

4. Discuss lessons 7 through 12. Choose one or more of the questions for reflection and discussion from each lesson to discuss as a group. You may want to ask group members which question was most challenging or helpful to them as you review each lesson.

5. Remember that there are no definitive answers for these discussion questions. The insights of group members will add to the understanding of all. None of these questions require an expert.

6. After talking about each lesson, instruct group members to complete lessons 13 through 18 on their own during the six days before the next group meeting. They should write out their own answers to the questions as preparation for next week's group discussion.

7. Ask the group if anyone is having any particular problems with the Bible study during the week. You may want to share advice and encouragement.

8. Conclude by praying aloud together the prayer at the end of one of the lessons discussed. You may add to the prayer based on the sharing that has occurred in the group.

"Blessed are the merciful, for they will receive mercy." MATT 5:7

The Beatitudes
on the Mountain

MATTHEW 5:1-10 *¹When Jesus saw the crowds, he went up the mountain; and after he sat down, his disciples came to him. ²Then he began to speak, and taught them, saying:*

³"Blessed are the poor in spirit, for theirs is the kingdom of heaven.

⁴"Blessed are those who mourn, for they will be comforted.

⁵"Blessed are the meek, for they will inherit the earth.

⁶"Blessed are those who hunger and thirst for righteousness, for they will be filled.

⁷"Blessed are the merciful, for they will receive mercy.

⁸"Blessed are the pure in heart, for they will see God.

⁹"Blessed are the peacemakers, for they will be called children of God.

¹⁰"Blessed are those who are persecuted for righteousness' sake, for theirs is the kingdom of heaven."

The Torah and prophets have demonstrated that the principal characteristic of God in relationship to God's people is mercy. On the mountain the Lord proclaimed to Moses the heart of God's self-revelation to Israel: "The Lord, a God merciful and gracious, slow to anger, and abounding in steadfast love and faithfulness" (Exod 34:6). Compassion, tenderness, faithful love, and forgiveness are the central features of the kingdom that the prophets have declared God wants to bring upon the earth.

Matthew's gospel presents Jesus on a mountain at the beginning of his ministry, delivering the inaugural address of God's kingdom. This Sermon on the Mount offers a condensed summary of the core of Jesus' teachings about living under God's reign. Jesus does not offer a new Torah or a new legal code. Rather, he declares his authoritative interpretation of Israel's Torah as one who embodies God's mercy. Jesus offers these Beatitudes as eight pillars of a lifestyle lived under God's merciful reign.

The eight Beatitudes name the key character traits of those who are "blessed" by God. These eight characteristics are evidence of God's gracious gifts offered to those responding to the message of the kingdom. These gifts, embodied in the life of Jesus and offered to those choosing to follow him, must be cultivated in the lifelong process of discipleship so that they become increasingly active in one's life.

Each of these eight characteristics of blessedness is followed by the promises of God. The first and the last Beatitude are followed by the words "for theirs is the kingdom of heaven." This present tense means that the experience of God's kingdom begins now in this life and will be perfected in the next. The other six Beatitudes are followed by verbs in the future tense, describing what God will do for them. Yet each of these describes an aspect of living in God's kingdom. The present experience of God's reign in the person of Jesus motivates the disciple to live in hopeful confidence of the future fullness.

The first four Beatitudes are qualities that describe our relationship with God. The "poor in spirit" are those who admit their poverty and acknowledge their total dependence on God. Those who cultivate this trust in God will begin experiencing the kingdom in their present lives and await its full realization (verse 3). "Those who mourn" are those who lament their own sins as well as the sin of the world. The mourning that results from afflictions and persecution will be met with God's future comfort (verse 4). The "meek" are those who possess an unassuming humility, based on the model of Jesus. These will ultimately inherit the earth, rather than those stocked with wealth, status, and arms (verse 5). "Those who hunger and thirst for righteousness" realize their lack of right behavior before God and desire that righteousness permeate society and culture. This deep desire for God's will to be done on earth will be satisfied with the full coming of God's kingdom (verse 6).

The second four Beatitudes are qualities that describe our relationship with other people. Those who are "merciful" in relationship to other people demonstrate compassion and loving kindness modeled on the life and teachings of Jesus. Those who deal mercifully with others will receive God's ultimate mercy and obtain the promises of his faithful love (verse 7). Those who are "pure in heart" possess an internal integrity and single-heartedness that manifests itself in both their private and public lives (verse 8). The "peacemakers" are those who actively seek harmonious relationships with others. Their experience of peace with God enables them to strive for the cessation of hostilities and active reconciliation between people, while awaiting God's ultimate peace to come upon the world (verse 9). Persecution "for righteousness' sake" is what those seeking to live the values taught by Jesus can expect to experience, but these will ultimately experience the fullness of God's kingdom. This second assurance of "the kingdom of heaven" brings the Beatitudes full circle (verse 10).

The lives of those living in God's kingdom are marked by humility toward God and mercy toward others. Because we have experienced such mercy from our God, we are required to promote a culture of mercy around us. This lifestyle of mercy is not something imposed from above; rather, it is a result of a connection with God and with those around us. In our acts of mercy, God's mercy becomes concretely realized. Those who live in this way are blessed indeed.

Reflection and Discussion

- The Beatitudes convince us that God's approval of our lives does not result from simply keeping a prescribed set of rules. What is necessary for living according to God's will?

- The Beatitudes demonstrate that those who comfortably fit in with society without causing trouble are not the people who are pleasing to God. In what sense are the Beatitudes countercultural?

- Which of these eight characteristics of kingdom living is most evident in my own life?

- How does being merciful lead to a fuller experience of God's mercy?

Prayer

Good Teacher, you guide your disciples to understand the lifestyle of those participating in God's kingdom. Transform me into the kind of person described by the Beatitudes so that I may follow in your way and live life with true happiness and blessedness.

**If God so clothes the grass of the field,
which is alive today and tomorrow is thrown into
the oven, will he not much more clothe you—
you of little faith?** MATT 6:30

God Cares for All of Your Needs

MATTHEW 6:25-34 ²⁵*"Therefore I tell you, do not worry about your life, what you will eat or what you will drink, or about your body, what you will wear. Is not life more than food, and the body more than clothing?* ²⁶*Look at the birds of the air; they neither sow nor reap nor gather into barns, and yet your heavenly Father feeds them. Are you not of more value than they?* ²⁷*And can any of you by worrying add a single hour to your span of life?* ²⁸*And why do you worry about clothing? Consider the lilies of the field, how they grow; they neither toil nor spin,* ²⁹*yet I tell you, even Solomon in all his glory was not clothed like one of these.* ³⁰*But if God so clothes the grass of the field, which is alive today and tomorrow is thrown into the oven, will he not much more clothe you—you of little faith?* ³¹*Therefore do not worry, saying, 'What will we eat?' or 'What will we drink?' or 'What will we wear?'* ³²*For it is the Gentiles who strive for all these things; and indeed your heavenly Father knows that you need all these things.* ³³*But strive first for the kingdom of God and his righteousness, and all these things will be given to you as well.*

³⁴*"So do not worry about tomorrow, for tomorrow will bring worries of its own. Today's trouble is enough for today."*

A s Jesus continues his Sermon on the Mount, he teaches us that in order to live a life characterized by God's mercy, we must trust in God's merciful care for us. He offers, first, a general command: "Do not worry about your life, what you will eat or what you will drink, or about your body, what you will wear." This kind of worry is not the ordinary concern we must have about life's necessities. Rather, it is undue anxiety that does not trust the Father's loving care for us. The command is followed by a rhetorical question asking whether life is not more than food and the body more than clothing. The response should be "of course," knowing that God who gives life will certainly supply the means to sustain it.

Jesus' command, "Do not worry," is followed by his exhortation to observe the birds of the air (verse 26). They do not grow their food, let alone grow anxious about it, but the Father gives them all the food they need. This encouragement to reflect on God's providential care for the birds is followed by another rhetorical question. Jesus asks whether we are not more valuable than they. Knowing that we are made in God's image, surely God will provide for all that we need. A follow-up rhetorical question asks if we can add to our life span by worrying (verse 28). Of course we can't, and we know today that anxiety and stress will surely shorten the span of our lives.

Jesus' encouragement to observe the birds of the air is followed by his exhortation to consider the lilies of the field. He shifts the focus here from food to clothing. These flowers do not create their clothing, yet they are more wondrously dressed than King Solomon in all his royal splendor. The rhetorical question leads Jesus' listeners to reflect on God's wonderful providence. If God cares so much for plants, which have such a brief life span, surely God will provide the clothing we need for our bodies (verse 30). Hesitation to trust God for all of our needs is due to our "little faith." This gentle rebuke is directed to followers whose faith is real but faltering. It is Jesus' way of saying, "Trust in God. Don't let your worries keep you from believing that God will provide for you. Deepening your faith will lessen your anxiety and provide you with a fuller life."

In essence, Jesus tells the crowd on the mountain and all his future disciples to put first things first: God's kingdom must be the primary concern of disciples (verse 33). Excessively worrying about the future only marginalizes God and the priorities of his kingdom from our lives. Tomorrow's food and clothing should not be our focus. Disciples must address themselves to the matters at hand today while trusting that tomorrow is in the hands of our loving Father. In this way the ordinary planning and work required for our daily needs will not be motivated by, or lead to, the anxieties that distract us from our allegiance to God's kingdom.

Reflection and Discussion

- What are the issues about which I worry excessively? Why does such worry express a failure to trust in God's care for me?

- How can reflecting on the birds of the air and lilies of the field help me to trust more in God's merciful love?

- What does Jesus urge us to put first in our lives? How can this priority adjustment help me to live a life with less anxiety and more quality?

Prayer

Heavenly Father, you keep the birds and the flowers in existence and provide for their daily needs. Free me from needless anxiety as I seek to make my first priority the concerns of your kingdom and the things that last forever.

"Go and learn what this means, 'I desire mercy, not sacrifice.'
For I have come to call not the righteous but sinners." MATT 9:13

Have Mercy on Us, Son of David

MATTHEW 9:9-13 ⁹*As Jesus was walking along, he saw a man called Matthew sitting at the tax booth; and he said to him, "Follow me." And he got up and followed him.*

¹⁰And as he sat at dinner in the house, many tax collectors and sinners came and were sitting with him and his disciples.¹¹When the Pharisees saw this, they said to his disciples, "Why does your teacher eat with tax collectors and sinners?" ¹²But when he heard this, he said, "Those who are well have no need of a physician, but those who are sick. ¹³Go and learn what this means, 'I desire mercy, not sacrifice.' For I have come to call not the righteous but sinners."

MATTHEW 9:27-31 ²⁷*As Jesus went on from there, two blind men followed him, crying loudly, "Have mercy on us, Son of David!" ²⁸When he entered the house, the blind men came to him; and Jesus said to them, "Do you believe that I am able to do this?" They said to him, "Yes, Lord." ²⁹Then he touched their eyes and said, "According to your faith let it be done to you." ³⁰And their eyes were opened. Then Jesus sternly ordered them, "See that no one knows of this." ³¹But they went away and spread the news about him throughout that district.*

The calling of Matthew is presented in the gospel within the context of divine mercy. The job of tax collector in the Roman system was awarded to the highest bidder. So while the collector was responsible for paying a set amount to the government, he would try to collect extra taxes from the people to increase his personal profits. For this reason, the tax collectors were despised as corrupt and dishonest collaborators with the Roman overseers. As Jesus was passing by the tax collector's booth, Jesus looked intently at Matthew with a look full of mercy. Jesus' invitation was compelling and direct, and Matthew's response was without hesitation.

The lifestyle of Jesus and his disciples—eating with "tax collectors and sinners"—was severely protested by some of the Pharisees (verse 11). Sharing a meal, in the Jewish culture, implies a close relationship. Jesus' compassionate eating with the outcasts became a hallmark of his ministry. Jesus' response to his opponents takes the form of a saying: "Those who are well have no need of a physician, but those who are sick" (verse 12). Jesus suggests that his ministry is like the healing of a physician. His merciful association with sinners is equivalent to the salvation he brings through his healings. He provides the medicine of mercy to the sinners in need of a restored wholeness. Like his physical healings, which bring the sick persons from their isolation and exclusion, Jesus brings sinners into the community of faith and includes them in his ministry.

In response to their protests, Jesus tells the Pharisees to reflect on the words of Hosea 6:6, "I desire mercy, not sacrifice" (verse 13). The text of the prophet prioritizes compassion over the performance of ritual sacrifice. Jesus cites the prophet in order to demonstrate that his ministry to tax collectors and sinners is in accord with the teachings of Scripture and thus not opposed to God's will. Like the prophets before him, Jesus does not advocate abolishing the temple or downplay its sacrificial system, but he understands the greater priority of merciful forgiveness in religious practice.

Jesus exemplifies the ideal taught by the prophets. God relates to sinners with mercy, and God's primary desire is for his people to show mercy. Obedience to the law of Israel starts with a compassionate heart. By citing the ancient Scriptures, the gospel demonstrates that Jesus, and not his opponents, exemplifies authentic obedience to God's word.

The ministry of Jesus, the divine physician, is illustrated in his healing of the two blind men. Their cry to Jesus, "Have mercy on us, Son of David!" focuses his messianic power as Son of David on the medicine of his mercy. Like his association with sinners, his healing of their blindness is an act of mercy that ends their isolation, restores their wholeness, and brings them into the community of salvation. They immediately begin to evangelize by spreading the news about Jesus.

Reflection and Discussion

- How do Jesus' call of Matthew and his eating with tax collectors and sinners demonstrate his mission of mercy?

- Why does Jesus urge the Pharisees to study the words of the prophet, "I desire mercy, not sacrifice"? How is Jesus challenging his church today through this biblical text?

- How is Jesus' inclusion of sinners in his mission like his healing of the blind men? In what way do both of these demonstrate the work of the divine physician and his use of the medicine of mercy?

Prayer

Divine Physician, you extend the medicine of mercy to the outcasts, the sinners, and the sick. Thank you for looking upon me with mercy, for calling me to discipleship, and for bringing me into the community of salvation.

"I forgave you all that debt because you pleaded with me.
Should you not have had mercy on your fellow slave,
as I had mercy on you?" MATT 18:32-33

Parable of the Unmerciful Servant

MATTHEW 18:23-34 ²³*"For this reason the kingdom of heaven may be compared to a king who wished to settle accounts with his slaves.* ²⁴*When he began the reckoning, one who owed him ten thousand talents was brought to him;* ²⁵*and, as he could not pay, his lord ordered him to be sold, together with his wife and children and all his possessions, and payment to be made.* ²⁶*So the slave fell on his knees before him, saying, 'Have patience with me, and I will pay you everything.'* ²⁷*And out of pity for him, the lord of that slave released him and forgave him the debt.* ²⁸*But that same slave, as he went out, came upon one of his fellow slaves who owed him a hundred denarii; and seizing him by the throat, he said, 'Pay what you owe.'* ²⁹*Then his fellow slave fell down and pleaded with him, 'Have patience with me, and I will pay you.'* ³⁰*But he refused; then he went and threw him into prison until he would pay the debt.* ³¹*When his fellow slaves saw what had happened, they were greatly distressed, and they went and reported to their lord all that had taken place.* ³²*Then his lord summoned him and said to him, 'You wicked slave! I forgave you all that debt because you pleaded with me.* ³³*Should you not have had mercy on your fellow slave, as I had mercy on you?'* ³⁴*And in anger his lord handed him over to be tortured until he would pay his entire debt."*

T his parable of God's kingdom tells of God's overwhelming mercy toward us and our responsibility to extend mercy to others. In this three-part story, the king represents God, and the king's slaves represent God's people. The impact of the parable is found in its contrasts.

The first scene tells of a servant, perhaps an official of the king's court, who owes the king an astonishingly large amount of money. "Ten thousand talents" could be translated by the slang "zillions." It is an amount that could never be paid back, even in a thousand lifetimes. So the servant begged the king to be patient with him and to give him time. But instead of merely allowing the servant time to repay the huge debt, the king exhibits profound compassion for the servant's plight and forgives the entire debt (verse 27). Each of us, of course, is that slave who owes a staggering amount to God, whose forgiving mercy knows no bounds. There is no way to pay back the debt of humanity's accumulated sin, yet our merciful God has forgiven us completely.

In the second scene, that same servant whose debt was totally remitted now comes upon one of his fellow slaves who owed him a relatively small amount. "A hundred denarii" could be paid off with a few months of labor. When the servant demanded that he pay the debt, the fellow slave begged him to be patient with him and give him time to repay the debt. But the unmerciful servant threw him into prison (verse 30). He refused to do for the other even a small fraction of what the king had already done for him. He accepts mercy for himself but is unwilling to grant it to another.

The third scene illustrates what happened when his fellow slaves saw what the ruthless servant had done. They are aghast at such hypocrisy. Although he had been forgiven a debt that he could never repay, he refused to forgive a debt that could be easily repaid. The other servants inform the king what had happened, and the king becomes infuriated. Summoning the servant back to him, the king says, "Should you not have had mercy on your fellow slave, as I had mercy on you?" (verse 33). The angry king cancels his merciful decision and condemns the servant for his lack of forgiveness. In the end, the merciless servant is treated in the same way that he treated his fellow servant.

The parable contains a profound teaching. Jesus shows that mercy is not only an action of God toward us. It becomes a criterion for determining who God's people truly are. In a nutshell, we are called to show mercy because mercy has first been shown to us. For followers of Jesus, this is an imperative from which we cannot excuse ourselves. After we have received unlimited mercy from God, this fragile gift of mercy is placed into our hands. We must rid ourselves of heartlessness, violence, and vengeance, letting mercy characterize our lives.

We cannot presume that God will free us from sin if we are not willing to forgive others. We cannot hide or suppress Jesus' speeches about divine judgment out of a false understanding of his message about divine mercy. The biblical words of God's judgment are always connected with a repeated and urgent call to conversion. They offer again and again a last chance, made possible by God's mercy. But those who reject God's merciful rule are accordingly excluded from the kingdom. Those who wish to be part of that kingdom must imitate the generous mercy of its Lord.

Reflection and Discussion

- What is the impact of the king's question on me: "Should you not have had mercy on your fellow slave, as I had mercy on you?" What does it say to me about divine mercy and my call to be merciful?

- Mercy must not be confused with sentimental tolerance or condoning evil. How does the parable indicate that divine judgment is real and must never be taken lightly?

Prayer

Lord of the kingdom, I praise you for your generous mercy toward me.
Give me the grace to be generous and merciful toward others, so that on the day of judgment you will welcome me into your heavenly reign.

When they heard that Jesus was passing by, they shouted,
"Lord, have mercy on us, Son of David!" MATT 20:30

Jesus Is Moved with Compassion

MATTHEW 20:29-34 *²⁹As they were leaving Jericho, a large crowd followed him. ³⁰There were two blind men sitting by the roadside. When they heard that Jesus was passing by, they shouted, "Lord, have mercy on us, Son of David!" ³¹The crowd sternly ordered them to be quiet; but they shouted even more loudly, "Have mercy on us, Lord, Son of David!" ³²Jesus stood still and called them, saying, "What do you want me to do for you?" ³³They said to him, "Lord, let our eyes be opened." ³⁴Moved with compassion, Jesus touched their eyes. Immediately they regained their sight and followed him.*

In the Greek text of the gospel, we find the two blind men crying out, "*Kyrie, eleison*—Lord, have mercy" (verse 30). Is anyone more dependent on the help of others than blind beggars? Could anyone be more in need of mercy? When they call out to the Lord, they are crying to God who has come among them as the Son of David, the Messiah of Israel. The Lord Jesus Christ is the mediator of God's mercy.

As Jesus travels the last stage of his journey to Jerusalem, the two blind men are sitting by the side of the road. Knowing that Jesus is the messianic healer, they call out repeatedly, "Have mercy on us, Lord, Son of David!" The designation is well-known among the Jews as a messianic title, an indication that the coming Messiah would be a royal figure from the lineage of King David. The blind men's cry anticipates the acclamation of the crowd a few verses later, which narrate Jesus' entry into Jerusalem: "Hosanna to the Son of David! Blessed is the one who comes in the name of the Lord!"

When asked by Jesus what they desire, their response is an unassuming prayer, "Lord, let our eyes by opened" (verse 33). This healing of the blind men, coupled with the preceding account of the healing of two blind men (Matt 9:27-31) and Jesus' other miracles, indicates that the messianic age prophesied by Isaiah has begun in Jesus: "Then the eyes of the blind shall be opened, and the ears of the deaf unstopped; then the lame shall leap like a deer, and the tongue of the speechless sing for joy" (Isa 35:5-6). In the previous healing narrative, the focus of the account is on faith. Jesus asked, "Do you believe that I am able to do this?" They said to him, "Yes, Lord" (Matt 9:28). In this account, the emphasis is changed from the faith of the blind men to the mercy of the healer. Here the text says, "Moved with compassion, Jesus touched their eyes" (verse 34). After regaining their sight, they then followed Jesus to Jerusalem, where he would be sacrificed as the merciful Messiah in his atoning death for sins.

The cry of these blind men is echoed in the *Kyrie, eleison* of the Christian liturgy. It became an early Christian prayer for healing and for the forgiveness of sins. The chant may have been in use in the church's prayer in the late first century when Matthew wrote his gospel. At the beginning of the Eucharist, we place ourselves in the place of the blind men, pleading for the Lord's mercy, trusting that he will open our eyes and forgive our sins so that we can follow him.

Reflection and Discussion

- Consider the experience of the blind men when the Lord opened their eyes. In what way is this scene a helpful analogy to the experience of gaining the spiritual sight of faith?

- Imaginatively place yourself in the scene as one of the blind men. What do you experience and how do you respond?

- How deep is my desire to see and to follow the Lord? What can I learn from the example of the blind men?

- Early Christians employed the acclamation *Kyrie, eleison* in litanies. How does knowing the context of its usage in the gospels help me appreciate its chant in the liturgy today?

Prayer

Lord, have mercy! Alone, I have no ability to see truly or to rid myself of sin. Lord, let my eyes be opened. I cry out to you all the day. I trust in your compassion, and I wait for your mercy.

"Lord, when was it that we saw you hungry or thirsty or a stranger or naked or sick or in prison, and did not take care of you?"

MATT 25:44

The Corporal Works of Mercy

MATT 25:31-46 *³¹"When the Son of Man comes in his glory, and all the angels with him, then he will sit on the throne of his glory. ³²All the nations will be gathered before him, and he will separate people one from another as a shepherd separates the sheep from the goats, ³³and he will put the sheep at his right hand and the goats at the left. ³⁴Then the king will say to those at his right hand, 'Come, you that are blessed by my Father, inherit the kingdom prepared for you from the foundation of the world; ³⁵for I was hungry and you gave me food, I was thirsty and you gave me something to drink, I was a stranger and you welcomed me, ³⁶I was naked and you gave me clothing, I was sick and you took care of me, I was in prison and you visited me.' ³⁷Then the righteous will answer him, 'Lord, when was it that we saw you hungry and gave you food, or thirsty and gave you something to drink? ³⁸And when was it that we saw you a stranger and welcomed you, or naked and gave you clothing? ³⁹And when was it that we saw you sick or in prison and visited you?' ⁴⁰And the king will answer them, 'Truly I tell you, just as you did it to one of the least of these who are members of my family, you did it to me.' ⁴¹Then he will say to those at his left hand, 'You that are accursed, depart from me into the eternal fire prepared for the devil and his angels; ⁴²for I was hungry and you gave me no food, I was thirsty and you gave me nothing to drink, ⁴³I was a stranger and* *you did not welcome me, naked and you did not give me clothing, sick and in prison and you did not visit me.' ⁴⁴Then they also will answer, 'Lord, when was it that we saw you hungry or thirsty or a stranger or naked or sick or in prison, and did not take care of you?' ⁴⁵Then he will answer them, 'Truly I tell you, just as you did not do it to one of the least of these, you did not do it to me.' ⁴⁶And these will go away into eternal punishment, but the righteous into eternal life."*

In his final instruction before his passion, Jesus teaches his disciples about his glorious return and the final judgment. He describes himself as the glorious Son of Man who comes with all his angels and sits on his glorious throne. The scene describes a universal gathering of "all the nations." This messianic king acts as a shepherd, a common metaphor for royal rulers, and separates people as a shepherd separates sheep from goats. The king determines who will enter his kingdom, seemingly using a single standard for making his judgment.

Those on the king's right are those who are blessed by the Father and inherit the kingdom prepared for them (verse 34). Jesus declares them blessed because they helped him when he was hungry, thirsty, away from home, naked, sick, and imprisoned. The blessed ones express puzzlement and ask when they saw Jesus in need and helped him. Apparently they can remember doing acts of compassion for others, but they can't remember doing such deeds for Jesus. However, Jesus responds that their works of mercy were done for him whenever they did them for one of the least of his brothers or sisters.

Those on the king's left have committed an appalling sin of omission. Jesus declares that they turned their backs on him when he was hungry, thirsty, away from home, naked, sick, and imprisoned. These are just as perplexed as those who are blessed. They apparently do not deny their refusal to come to the aid of those in need, but they do not recall refusing to serve Jesus in his need. However, Jesus responds that their denial of help to one of the least of his brothers or sisters was a refusal to come to his aid.

If Jesus had not given us this explicit teaching about the last judgment, we would perhaps imagine the scene quite differently. We might expect to be judged on the basis of whether we obeyed all the commandments, on how faithfully we went to church, or how often we prayed. We might be more worried about how many sins we committed than what we omitted doing. And we might consider the works of mercy as optional extras in the Christian life. Jesus repeats the mention of those who are hungry, thirsty, away from home, naked, sick, and imprisoned a total of four times in this teaching. This repetition imprints these least ones on the minds of his listeners and certainly on the minds of those who listen to the gospel. No one reflecting on this account of the last judgment can have any doubt that Jesus wants his followers to show mercy to those in need. He stresses the everlasting significance of the decision whether or not to help the least ones. The blessed will experience inexpressible joy in God's presence forever, and the accursed will experience unspeakable horror in separation from God.

Of course, we shouldn't interpret Jesus' teaching on the last judgment to mean that none of his other requirements of us matter. But the fact that Jesus makes how we treat the least ones the criterion by which we will be judged means that these works of mercy are of paramount importance in his eyes. We cannot excuse our lack of mercy by claiming that we have obeyed the rest of the commandments. Jesus' teaching makes it quite clear that practicing mercy means performing deeds. We cannot just feel sad about the hungry; we must do something to feed them. We cannot just sympathize with the homeless; we must see that they are offered shelter. We cannot just feel frustrated at the plight of the immigrants and refugees; we must help to create a culture of mercy. Our experience of God's mercy obliges us to become ministers of mercy in the world.

Reflection and Discussion

- What are the common elements in all six of these works of mercy? What might be another work that Jesus might mention today?

- Jesus says that our sins of omission are those that most seriously inhibit our salvation. What is Jesus telling me not to omit from my life?

- In light of Jesus' judgment of the nations, how might his teaching challenge the priorities of my nation on poverty, nutrition, health care, prisons, or immigration?

- Which of these works of mercy could I perform this week for one of my brothers and sisters in need?

Prayer

King of all nations, you have taught me that whatever I do for those in need, I do for you. Open my eyes to see your presence in those who are hungry, thirsty, away from home, naked, sick, and imprisoned.

SUGGESTIONS FOR FACILITATORS, GROUP SESSION 4

1. Welcome group members and ask if anyone has any questions, announcements, or requests.

2. You may want to pray this prayer as a group:
   Compassionate Lord, you extend the medicine of mercy to the sick, the outcasts, and the sinners. Heal our blindness so that we may see your presence in those who are hungry, thirsty, away from home, naked, sick, and imprisoned. Free us from needless anxiety so that our first priority is the concerns of your kingdom. We wait for your mercy, and trust in your compassion. Make us generous and merciful toward others, and on the day of judgment, welcome us into your heavenly reign.

3. Ask one or more of the following questions:
   - What is the most difficult part of this study for you?
   - What insights stand out to you from the lessons this week?

4. Discuss lessons 13 through 18. Choose one or more of the questions for reflection and discussion from each lesson to discuss as a group. You may want to ask group members which question was most challenging or helpful to them as you review each lesson.

5. Keep the discussion moving, but allow time for the questions that provoke the most discussion. Encourage the group members to use "I" language in their responses.

6. After talking over each lesson, instruct group members to complete lessons 19 through 24 on their own during the six days before the next group meeting. They should write out their own answers to the questions as preparation for next week's session.

7. Ask the group what encouragement they need for the coming week. Ask the members to pray for the needs of one another during the week.

8. Conclude by praying aloud together the prayer at the end of one of the lessons discussed. You may choose to conclude the prayer by asking members to pray aloud any requests they may have.

Thus he has shown the mercy promised to our ancestors,
and has remembered his holy covenant, the oath that he swore
to our ancestor Abraham. LUKE 1:72-73

Song of God's Tender Mercy

LUKE 1:67-79 ⁶⁷*Then his father Zechariah was filled with the Holy Spirit and spoke this prophecy:*

⁶⁸*"Blessed be the Lord God of Israel,*
for he has looked favorably on his people and redeemed them.
⁶⁹*He has raised up a mighty savior for us*
in the house of his servant David,
⁷⁰*as he spoke through the mouth of his holy prophets from of old,*
⁷¹*that we would be saved from our enemies and from the hand of all who hate us.*
⁷²*Thus he has shown the mercy promised to our ancestors,*
and has remembered his holy covenant,
⁷³*the oath that he swore to our ancestor Abraham,*
to grant us ⁷⁴*that we, being rescued from the hands of our enemies,*
might serve him without fear, ⁷⁵*in holiness and righteousness*
before him all our days.
⁷⁶*And you, child, will be called the prophet of the Most High;*
for you will go before the Lord to prepare his ways,
⁷⁷*to give knowledge of salvation to his people*
by the forgiveness of their sins.

⁷⁸By the tender mercy of our God,
  the dawn from on high will break upon us,
⁷⁹to give light to those who sit in darkness and in the shadow of death,
  to guide our feet into the way of peace."

The opening chapter of Luke's gospel forms a transition from the old covenant to the new, from the Scriptures of Israel to the gospel of Jesus Christ. The figures of Zechariah, Elizabeth, and John the Baptist represent the people of the old covenant preparing the way for what God will do next. These words of Zechariah evoke the events of redemption that God has worked throughout the history of Israel. His prayer echoes the psalms and other prayers of Israel's Scriptures in light of the "mighty savior" God is raising up for them.

These words of Zechariah present a smooth movement from his ministry as a priest in the temple of Jerusalem to the birth of his son, John the Baptist. The prayer is directed to "the Lord God of Israel" whom the gospel will show to be the same God as the Father of Jesus. The opposition that some people maintain between the merciful God of the New Testament and the wrathful God of the Old Testament is nowhere to be found in Luke's gospel. In fact, as our Scriptures from the Torah, prophets, and psalms have indicated, the primary characteristic of the one God of both the old and the new covenant is mercy.

This prayer of praise calls upon God who "has shown the mercy promised to our ancestors" (verse 72). This divine mercy was first revealed to Abraham and embedded in "his holy covenant." Now this mercy is being fully revealed as God raises up the Messiah from the house of David for the work of redeeming the people. This is nothing less than a new "exodus" for God's people, as they are "rescued" from their enemies and liberated to serve and worship God "in holiness and righteousness" (verses 74-75).

The role of John the Baptist, as "the prophet of the Most High," is to prepare the way for God, who will come to his people through Jesus the Messiah. John heralds the arrival of God's salvation and the forgiveness of sins (verse 77). In contrast, Jesus is "the dawn" that comes from God, the one who will scatter the darkness of sin and death, who will guide God's people "into the way of peace" (verses 78-79). The Messiah's light refers to his coming to humanity, his teaching God's ways, and his ministry of salvation.

All of salvation history, culminating in the coming of Christ and all his wonderful works, is the manifestation of God's "tender mercy" (verse 78). This term in Greek means literally "bowels of mercy." It could also be translated as "compassionate mercy" or "heartfelt mercy." It expresses the reality that God is merciful from the inner depth of his being. Divine love, made known in countless ways through God's word, is filled with deep compassion for us.

Reflection and Discussion

- How does this prayer of Zechariah indicate that the God of the old covenant and of the new covenant is a God of mercy?

- In what sense do the words of Zechariah describe the mercy of God revealed in Jesus as a "new exodus," a new experience of the mercy God showed through freeing his people from slavery?

- In what ways have I experienced the "tender mercy" of God through these words of praise from Zechariah?

Prayer

Lord God of Israel, you have looked with favor upon us and revealed the mercy you promised to our ancestors. Thank you for the tender mercy you have shown through the coming of our Savior among us. May his light guide our feet in the way of your mercy.

"He has sent me to proclaim release to the captives and recovery of sight to the blind, to let the oppressed go free, to proclaim the year of the Lord's favor." LUKE 4:18-19

Jesus Announces His Ministry of Mercy

LUKE 4:14-21 ¹⁴*Then Jesus, filled with the power of the Spirit, returned to Galilee, and a report about him spread through all the surrounding country.* ¹⁵*He began to teach in their synagogues and was praised by everyone.*

¹⁶*When he came to Nazareth, where he had been brought up, he went to the synagogue on the sabbath day, as was his custom. He stood up to read,* ¹⁷*and the scroll of the prophet Isaiah was given to him. He unrolled the scroll and found the place where it was written:*

¹⁸*"The Spirit of the Lord is upon me,*
  because he has anointed me to bring good news to the poor.
He has sent me to proclaim release to the captives
  and recovery of sight to the blind, to let the oppressed go free,
¹⁹*to proclaim the year of the Lord's favor."*

²⁰*And he rolled up the scroll, gave it back to the attendant, and sat down. The eyes of all in the synagogue were fixed on him.* ²¹*Then he began to say to them, "Today this scripture has been fulfilled in your hearing."*

Jesus began his public ministry by teaching in the synagogues of Galilee. The synagogues, as the places where the Jewish people assemble for prayer, Scripture reading, instruction, and discussion, were the natural settings for Jesus to present his teachings to the people. Jesus was well versed in the Torah and prophets of Israel, and at these Sabbath gatherings he would read from the scrolls of Scripture and interpret God's word in light of his mission as Israel's Messiah.

This proclamation of Jesus in the synagogue of Nazareth serves as a kind of prologue to his saving ministry. It is his inaugural address for Luke's gospel, a purpose similar to that of his proclamation of the Beatitudes for Matthew's gospel. In both passages, Jesus serves as the teacher of God's people. The mountain of Matthew's gospel and the synagogue of Luke's gospel are both crucial settings where the word of God is publicly announced to God's people. The Sermon on the Mount in Matthew's gospel and this proclamation in the synagogue offer condensed summaries of the core of Jesus' teachings about living under God's reign.

Jesus begins by unrolling the scroll and reading from the prophet Isaiah. In the prophetic text, God's anointed one announces release to those held in bondage (Isa 61:1-2). This text of liberation echoes the exodus from Egypt, but it is far greater. The deliverance is marked by four infinitives: to bring good news to the poor, to proclaim liberty to captives and sight to the blind, to let the oppressed go free, and to proclaim the year of the Lord's favor.

The text of Isaiah includes two additional infinitives that are not included in Matthew's account: "to bind up the brokenhearted" and "to comfort all who mourn" (Isa 61:1-2). Clearly the passage describes how God's anointed one is commissioned to bring mercy to God's people. Those to whom God's mission of mercy is directed—the poor, captive, blind, oppressed, brokenhearted, and mourning—are those who understand their own deep needs. They respond more directly and honestly to God's message of hope than people who do not recognize their own need for God's mercy.

The imagery of liberation echoes the description of ancient Israel's Jubilee year, an extraordinary time in which debts were cancelled, property was distributed, and slaves were liberated (Lev 25:8-17). Jesus' announcement of "the year of the Lord's favor" indicates the arrival of the time when the spiritual debt of sin will be forgiven, justice will be done for the deprived, and those held in the bondage of sickness and evil will be freed.

The Jewish people at the time of Jesus understood that this passage from Isaiah refers to the coming of God's new age of salvation, so its proclamation by Jesus catches the attention of his listeners as they wait to hear his instructions. As Jesus sat down, the customary position for teaching, he begins with the words, "Today this scripture has been fulfilled in your hearing" (verse 21). He is stating that the total deliverance that the prophet has described is now put into motion with his coming as Messiah. Jesus himself is the one anointed with God's Spirit to be the bearer of God's salvation to his people. And the "today" of Jesus' mission must never be allowed to become "yesterday" or to slip into a vague "someday."

In summary, this reading and interpretation of the scroll of Isaiah serves as an announcement of who Jesus is, of what his ministry consists, and of what his church is called to be and do. To be sure, the words and deeds of Jesus throughout the rest of Luke's gospel demonstrate this mission of Jesus. And Luke's second volume of writing, the Acts of the Apostles, shows that this is the mission of his church. It is the mission of divine mercy.

Reflection and Discussion

• In what ways am I poor, captive, blind, oppressed, brokenhearted, and mourning? Do I truly believe that Jesus wants to grant me release from all that holds me captive?

• In what ways does Jesus' proclamation from the scroll of Isaiah broaden my understanding of his salvation to include healing, forgiveness, and liberation?

- In what sense is the ministry of Jesus like an extended Jubilee year, "the year of the Lord's favor"?

- In what ways does Luke show us that Jesus' mission of mercy is now the mission of his church?

- Jesus says to those listening to him, "Today this scripture has been fulfilled in your hearing," but the New Testament shows that this "today" becomes an everlasting "now." How do these words of Jesus give me hope?

Prayer

*Lord God, your Son Jesus announced good news to the poor, captive, blind,
and oppressed. Open my life to accept your liberating word and to receive
the salvation that you give to all people who recognize their need and turn to you.*

> "If you love those who love you, what credit is that to you?
> If you do good to those who do good to you,
> what credit is that to you?" LUKE 6:32-33

Be Merciful as Your Father Is Merciful

LUKE 6:27-36 *27"But I say to you that listen, Love your enemies, do good to those who hate you, 28bless those who curse you, pray for those who abuse you. 29If anyone strikes you on the cheek, offer the other also; and from anyone who takes away your coat do not withhold even your shirt. 30Give to everyone who begs from you; and if anyone takes away your goods, do not ask for them again. 31Do to others as you would have them do to you.*

32"If you love those who love you, what credit is that to you? For even sinners love those who love them. 33If you do good to those who do good to you, what credit is that to you? For even sinners do the same. 34If you lend to those from whom you hope to receive, what credit is that to you? Even sinners lend to sinners, to receive as much again. 35But love your enemies, do good, and lend, expecting nothing in return. Your reward will be great, and you will be children of the Most High; for he is kind to the ungrateful and the wicked. 36Be merciful, just as your Father is merciful."

Because God has shown such immeasurable mercy to us, then we ought to at least reflect that mercy in our relationships with others. The love that a disciple is called to demonstrate must be greater than worldly standards of love. It means loving without strings attached, going the extra step, and demonstrating compassion. In fact, our ultimate judgment depends on the quality of our mercy.

Jesus' exhortation that his followers live a life of merciful love begins with four radical imperatives. "Love your enemies" is matchless in its emphatic and countercultural weight. "Do good to those who hate you" specifies that the love of enemies requires concrete deeds on behalf of those who oppose us. "Bless those who curse you" moves from deeds to words, even asking favor from God for our enemies. "Pray for those who abuse you" requires that we even intercede before God for those who oppose us. These four expressions of mercy toward enemies require that we reverse our natural inclinations to retaliate. Such supernatural love can only be generated within us when we have become deeply conscious of God's mercy. Such love is an imitation of God.

Next, Jesus offers four illustrations of love for enemies (verses 29-30). If given an insulting slap on the cheek, "offer the other also." The natural instinct is to slap in return, but Jesus excludes revenge. We must continue caring even when insulted, persist in serving even when persecuted, keep on doing good even when affronted, and remain vulnerable to insult again. If anyone takes away your coat, don't withhold even your shirt. Jesus rejects the logic of giving in order to get something in return. Rather, he urges us to go beyond what is required or demanded, to give and keep on giving. For us to "give to anyone" who requests basic human needs, we must give without considering whether the beneficiary is worthy of our gift. The fourth illustration urges us not to seek retribution. Even if someone takes what we have, we must be willing to part with it in a generous self-denial. Jesus is demonstrating that the principle of love for enemies reaches into many areas of life. We could summarize these illustrations by saying that Jesus urges us to show mercy and generosity to the enemy to such a degree that the enemy may even become a friend. Our concern must not be hatred, revenge, or payback, but the good of the other and a desire to win them over to the side of mercy.

The next imperative, "Do to others as you would have them do to you," seems, on the surface, to be a nice rule about reciprocity, an exchange for mutual benefit (verse 31). Other figures offer similar teachings. Confucius said, "What you do not want done to yourself, do not do to others." Rabbi Hillel said, "What is hateful to you, do not do to your neighbor." Yet, the illustrations that follow show that Jesus is not at all talking about a reciprocal way of doing things (verses 32-33). If you "love those who love you," "do good to those who do good to you," and "lend to those from whom you hope to receive," there is nothing particularly noteworthy about that. Everyone in the world holds this as a general principle of life. The life of a follower of Jesus demands a higher standard. The loving, doing good, and lending for us must be done without a hidden agenda, without strings attached, without seeking a reward. Such acts of mercy must be done with a heart for the other.

By living in this way, disciples show themselves as "children of the Most High" (verse 35). As children imitate their parents, when we live the life of mercy, we imitate God. As God is "kind to the ungrateful and the wicked," when we do the same, we are living as God's children, reflecting divine mercy to the world. In summary, God's character must be the guide for our character. As Jesus exhorts, "Be merciful, just as your Father is merciful." Living in God's kingdom means loving as God loves, caring for others as God cares for them, giving generously as God gives, forgiving others as God forgives. The mercy of God is both the source and the motivation of our deeds as disciples of Jesus.

Reflection and Discussion

- Read Proverbs 24:17 and 25:21-22. In what ways are these verses contrary to my impressions of the Old Testament? How do they prepare for Jesus' command to "love your enemies"?

- In what sense is the common practice of doing good to others so that they will do good to you inadequate for a follower of Jesus? What more is required?

- How can I live out the four radical imperatives contained in verses 27-28?

- How can I apply the four illustrations of verses 29-30 to my own life? What should motivate my responses?

- Why can we say that Jesus' exhortation "Be merciful, just as your Father is merciful" summarizes this section of his teaching on mercy?

Prayer

God Most High, you are merciful even to the wicked and ungrateful. Work deeply within my heart so that your mercy increasingly becomes the source and motivation for all that I do. Help me to love my enemies and to imitate you in showing compassion.

He went to him and bandaged his wounds, having poured oil and wine on them. Then he put him on his own animal, brought him to an inn, and took care of him. LUKE 10:34

The One Who Showed Him Mercy

LUKE 10:25-37 ²⁵*Just then a lawyer stood up to test Jesus. "Teacher," he said, "what must I do to inherit eternal life?" ²⁶He said to him, "What is written in the law? What do you read there?" ²⁷He answered, "You shall love the Lord your God with all your heart, and with all your soul, and with all your strength, and with all your mind; and your neighbor as yourself." ²⁸And he said to him, "You have given the right answer; do this, and you will live."*

²⁹*But wanting to justify himself, he asked Jesus, "And who is my neighbor?" ³⁰Jesus replied, "A man was going down from Jerusalem to Jericho, and fell into the hands of robbers, who stripped him, beat him, and went away, leaving him half dead. ³¹Now by chance a priest was going down that road; and when he saw him, he passed by on the other side. ³²So likewise a Levite, when he came to the place and saw him, passed by on the other side. ³³But a Samaritan while traveling came near him; and when he saw him, he was moved with pity. ³⁴He went to him and bandaged his wounds, having poured oil and wine on them. Then he put him on his own animal, brought him to an inn, and took care of him. ³⁵The next day he took out two denarii, gave them to the innkeeper, and said, 'Take care of him; and when I come back, I will repay you whatever more you spend.' ³⁶Which of these three, do you think, was a neighbor to the man who fell into the hands of the robbers?" ³⁷He said, "The one who showed him mercy." Jesus said to him, "Go and do likewise."*

Jesus expounds for us the message of God's mercy in many of his parables, but none so beautifully as in his parable of the good Samaritan. When the Samaritan sees the wounded one on the roadside, he is moved with compassion for him. He forgets the matters of the day for which he was on the move, lowers himself to the victim, and tends to his wounds. Next, the Samaritan puts the wounded one on his own donkey, takes him to the inn, and nurses him through the night. The next day he generously pays the inn-keeper in advance and leaves to finish his business in the city, but pledges to return.

Jesus tells this parable in response to the lawyer's question: "And who is my neighbor?" (verse 29). The parable demonstrates that the neighbor is the one for whom we become the neighbor, the one whom we physically encounter in a particular situation of need. The essence of being a neighbor is having the sensitivity to see a person experiencing hardship and acting to meet the need. As illustrated in the parable, the answer to the question, "And who is my neighbor?" is "the one who showed him mercy" (verse 37).

The power and shock of this parable, in light of Jesus' teachings on mercy, is the fact that the "neighbor" is the "enemy." The one who showed mercy is a member of the people most despised by the Jewish people. The Samaritans were avoided by the Jews, who considered them a heretical sect that had in-termarried with foreign peoples. So, not only did the Samaritan treat the man on the side of the road with tender mercy, he did so at great personal risk. In telling this parable, in which a Samaritan is the model to be imitated, Jesus demonstrates that love for neighbor is gauged solely according to the concrete suffering of the person whom we meet on the way.

In asking the question, "And who is my neighbor?" the lawyer wanted to determine the minimal response necessary to comply with the law command-ing love of neighbor. In ancient Israel, the "neighbor" was a fellow country-man, a member of the covenant. The lawyer knows that if loving his neighbor is the way to life, he wants as few neighbors as possible that he would be re-quired to love. But, as the parable makes clear, neighborliness is not found in racial, religious, or national bonds. It is found in every concrete expression of need and help.

The original question to Jesus in this passage comes from the lawyer: "What must I do to inherit eternal life?" The lawyer assumed that eternal life is something that must be earned. But eternal life is, sure enough, like an inheritance. An inheritance is something that is given to us. Yet there can be conditions attached to receiving an inheritance. Jesus draws out these conditions, and he affirmed the lawyer's response from Israel's Torah. We must love God totally (Deut 6:5) and love our neighbor as ourselves (Lev 19:18).

Jesus builds on the ancient teachings of Israel and expands them. Loving God and loving our neighbor go hand in hand, but our neighbor is anyone in need of help. Our motivation for loving is not earning eternal life; rather, it is extending the mercy we have received from God. The experience of God's merciful love for us encourages and obliges us to become witnesses of mercy and to deploy our lives on behalf of mercy in the world. We are commanded, along with the lawyer, to "go and do likewise," to go and be merciful.

Reflection and Discussion

- In what ways am I like the priest and Levite of the parable? What does the Samaritan teach me?

- What is the significance of the fact that the "neighbor" is the "enemy" in Jesus' parable? What is the challenge this offers to me?

Prayer

Compassionate Lord, you call me to love my neighbor, even when my neighbor is an enemy. As you have been merciful to me, help me to extend mercy to others. Give me the grace to be merciful today to all to whom you call me to be a neighbor.

"I tell you, there will be more joy in heaven over one sinner who repents than over ninety-nine righteous persons who need no repentance." LUKE 15:7

Jesus Has Come to Save the Lost

LUKE 15:1-10   ¹*Now all the tax collectors and sinners were coming near to listen to him. ²And the Pharisees and the scribes were grumbling and saying, "This fellow welcomes sinners and eats with them."*

³So he told them this parable: ⁴"Which one of you, having a hundred sheep and losing one of them, does not leave the ninety-nine in the wilderness and go after the one that is lost until he finds it? ⁵When he has found it, he lays it on his shoulders and rejoices. ⁶And when he comes home, he calls together his friends and neighbors, saying to them, 'Rejoice with me, for I have found my sheep that was lost.' ⁷Just so, I tell you, there will be more joy in heaven over one sinner who repents than over ninety-nine righteous persons who need no repentance.

⁸"Or what woman having ten silver coins, if she loses one of them, does not light a lamp, sweep the house, and search carefully until she finds it? ⁹When she has found it, she calls together her friends and neighbors, saying, 'Rejoice with me, for I have found the coin that I had lost.' ¹⁰Just so, I tell you, there is joy in the presence of the angels of God over one sinner who repents."

These parables of Jesus are a response to the outrage of the Pharisees and scribes, who are upset that Jesus spends time with sinners and eats with them. Yet Jesus never excluded anyone from his presence and even has a special affection for the poor and outcasts. His fondness for the outsider is reciprocated, and Luke introduces this section of his gospel by noting that "all the tax collectors and sinners were coming near to listen to him." In these parables, Jesus explains why he welcomes and cares for sinners.

The first parable tells of a shepherd who is trying to account for all his sheep and discovers that one is missing. The shepherd leaves the rest of his flock and gives his undivided attention to seeking the lost one. His search continues until he locates the animal, places it on his shoulders, and brings it home rejoicing. Considering that the sheep could have been stolen or destroyed by wild animals, the shepherd calls his friends and neighbors together to celebrate his find.

Jesus' application points out that the parable describes the heart of God for sinners. There is great rejoicing in heaven over the repentance of one sinner. In fact, God expresses greater joy over one repentant sinner than over ninety-nine righteous people. The possibility of finding the lost is the reason why Jesus "welcomes sinners and eats with them." He urges disciples to share in his passionate desire to seek the lost.

The second parable tells of a woman who discovers that one of her silver coins is lost. Although the drachma represents only a modest amount of money, the woman proceeds on a thorough search. She lights a lamp to help her see and sweeps the house with a broom, hoping to brush it out of some corner or hear its sound on the floor. She searches diligently until she finds the lost coin. Then she calls her female friends and neighbors to celebrate the find with her.

The two parables are almost exactly parallel. They both describe a relentless search for what is lost and express irresistible joy at the find. God is like the shepherd and the woman. The point of each story is that God will go to great efforts and rejoice with great joy to find and reconcile a sinner. In a culture where tax collectors are despised and sinners are shunned, Jesus offers teachings that encourage the rejected to come to him. His response to wayward people is strongly contrasted with that of the grumbling religious leaders. Jesus is the model for his disciples. Their mission, like that of Jesus, is to love people and draw them to God. They must reflect his concern and compassion, seeking out the lost and rejoicing with the heavens over every repentant sinner.

Reflection and Discussion

- In what ways do the compassionate shepherd and the determined woman represent God?

- Using my imagination to visualize these two scenes, how do the parables make me feel about my value to God?

- Why would these parables be particularly attractive to those who are shunned and rejected? In what sense am I the lost sheep and the lost coin?

Prayer

Merciful and relentless God, you have searched for me and found me. Give me a heart for the lost of our world, and let me rejoice with you over every repentant person who enters your embrace.

"God, I thank you that I am not like other people: thieves, rogues, adulterers, or even like this tax collector. I fast twice a week; I give a tenth of all my income." LUKE 18:11-12

God, Be Merciful to Me, a Sinner

LUKE 18:9-14 *⁹He also told this parable to some who trusted in themselves that they were righteous and regarded others with contempt: ¹⁰"Two men went up to the temple to pray, one a Pharisee and the other a tax collector. ¹¹The Pharisee, standing by himself, was praying thus, 'God, I thank you that I am not like other people: thieves, rogues, adulterers, or even like this tax collector. ¹²I fast twice a week; I give a tenth of all my income.' ¹³But the tax collector, standing far off, would not even look up to heaven, but was beating his breast and saying, 'God, be merciful to me, a sinner!' ¹⁴I tell you, this man went down to his home justified rather than the other; for all who exalt themselves will be humbled, but all who humble themselves will be exalted."*

This parable contrasts the prayer of the Pharisee and the tax collector. If we remember that the Pharisees at the time of Jesus were seen as the models of religious learning and devotion while tax collectors were despised as corrupt collaborators with the Roman occupiers, we can better comprehend the impact of Jesus' story. When these two men went up to the temple to pray, the differences in their internal dispositions are obvious. The Pharisee knew that he was keeping the commandments and carefully carrying out his religious duties (verses 11-12). Assuming himself to be righteous before God, he didn't pray for God's mercy. In fact, he thanked God that he did not need to rely on God's mercy, grateful that he was not like the tax collector standing nearby. He is pleased with all that he does for God and has no real sense of his own sinfulness and unworthiness before the Lord.

In contrast, the tax collector humbles himself, confesses that he is a sinner, and cries out for God's mercy (verse 13). He makes no comparison with others, and he knows that the only way to improve his relationship with God is to rely on the Lord's merciful grace. He prayed like the blind man begging to be healed, simply crying out for God's mercy.

Jesus concludes the parable by stating that the tax collector, not the Pharisee, went home justified before God. What the Pharisee strove to achieve through his own efforts, the tax collector received as God's gift. The story of the Pharisee is not told by Jesus so that we can feel superior to him, but so that we don't tragically fall into his error. Those of us who live upright lives and follow the rules of faith need divine mercy just as much as anyone else. The story of the tax collector is held up by Jesus as our example. He simply asks for and relies on God's mercy.

Jesus teaches that people can never earn or deserve salvation. The grace of God's merciful forgiveness shows that no one can feel religiously superior to another. The parable's conclusion warns disciples not to exalt themselves before God lest they be humbled. Again, Jesus shows how God honors humility and reverses human expectations. Prayer should be unassuming and honest, not trying to convince God of our righteousness but acknowledging our dependence on his grace and mercy.

Reflection and Discussion

- Jesus tells this parable so that we don't fall into the tragic error of the Pharisee. What traits of the Pharisee sometimes characterize my life?

- What do I see of myself in each of these two characters?

- What characteristics of the tax collector is Jesus urging me to imitate?

- If Jesus told this parable today in order to communicate the same point, what group of people would be the Pharisee and who would be the tax collector?

- What should I do if I tend to feel religiously superior to another person?

Prayer

Lord, be merciful to me, a sinner. I come before you, grateful for your gift of forgiveness and salvation. Help me to confidently trust in your grace.

SUGGESTIONS FOR FACILITATORS, GROUP SESSION 5

1. Welcome group members and ask if anyone has any questions, announcements, or requests.

2. You may want to pray this prayer as a group:
   Lord God, you are merciful even to the wicked and ungrateful, and you call us to love our neighbor, even where our neighbor is an enemy. Extend your grace into our hearts so that your mercy increasingly becomes the source and motivation of all we do. Give us compassion for the lost and a desire to extend your mercy to them. Lord, be merciful to us sinners, and help us confidently trust in your gift of forgiveness and salvation.

3. Ask one or more of the following questions:
   - What most intrigued you from this week's study?
   - Why is Luke's gospel often considered the good news of mercy and compassion?

4. Discuss lessons 19 through 24. Choose one or more of the questions for reflection and discussion from each lesson to talk over as a group.

5. Ask the group members to name one thing they have most appreciated about the way the group has worked during this Bible study. Ask group members to discuss any changes they might suggest in the way the group works in future studies.

6. Invite group members to complete lessons 25 through 30 on their own during the six days before the next meeting. They should write out their own answers to the questions as preparation for next week's session.

7. Discuss ways in which God's mercy is expressed in contemporary film, art, or culture.

8. Conclude by praying aloud together the prayer at the end of one of the lessons discussed. You may want to conclude the prayer by asking members to voice prayers of thanksgiving.

Rejoice in hope, be patient in suffering, persevere in prayer.
Contribute to the needs of the saints; extend hospitality
to strangers. ROM 12:12-13

The Marks of a Merciful Christian

ROMANS 12:1-21 *¹I appeal to you therefore, brothers and sisters, by the mercies of God, to present your bodies as a living sacrifice, holy and acceptable to God, which is your spiritual worship. ²Do not be conformed to this world, but be transformed by the renewing of your minds, so that you may discern what is the will of God—what is good and acceptable and perfect.*

³For by the grace given to me I say to everyone among you not to think of yourself more highly than you ought to think, but to think with sober judgment, each according to the measure of faith that God has assigned. ⁴For as in one body we have many members, and not all the members have the same function, ⁵so we, who are many, are one body in Christ, and individually we are members one of another. ⁶We have gifts that differ according to the grace given to us: prophecy, in proportion to faith; ⁷ministry, in ministering; the teacher, in teaching; ⁸the exhorter, in exhortation; the giver, in generosity; the leader, in diligence; the compassionate, in cheerfulness.

⁹Let love be genuine; hate what is evil, hold fast to what is good; ¹⁰love one another with mutual affection; outdo one another in showing honor. ¹¹Do not lag in zeal, be ardent in spirit, serve the Lord. ¹²Rejoice in hope, be patient in suffering, persevere in prayer. ¹³Contribute to the needs of the saints; extend hospitality to strangers.

101

¹⁴Bless those who persecute you; bless and do not curse them. ¹⁵Rejoice with those who rejoice, weep with those who weep. ¹⁶Live in harmony with one another; do not be haughty, but associate with the lowly; do not claim to be wiser than you are. ¹⁷Do not repay anyone evil for evil, but take thought for what is noble in the sight of all. ¹⁸If it is possible, so far as it depends on you, live peaceably with all. ¹⁹Beloved, never avenge yourselves, but leave room for the wrath of God; for it is written, "Vengeance is mine, I will repay, says the Lord." ²⁰No, "if your enemies are hungry, feed them; if they are thirsty, give them something to drink; for by doing this you will heap burning coals on their heads." ²¹Do not be overcome by evil, but overcome evil with good.

In this letter Paul summons his readers to a pattern of living that corresponds to the gospel of Jesus Christ that they have received. The mercy we have received from God is not an abstraction, but a gift that gives shape and direction for Christian living. Paul exhorts us to present our lives as "a living sacrifice, holy and acceptable to God" (verse 1). The imagery he uses is that of the sacrifices offered to God in the temple of Jerusalem. Like those sacrifices, we ought to offer all that we say and do as a living sacrifice, a holy offering in worship of God. If God has redeemed our whole life through divine mercy, then the only fitting response is the offering of our whole existence in devotion to God.

In order to live the Christian life as a sacrificial consecration to God, Paul insists that his readers not be "conformed" to the world with all its superficial and passing attractions, but be "transformed" by the power of grace to live in a new way of life (verse 2). God's transforming grace renews our minds, giving us the power to discern what is necessary to live according to "the will of God" in the often difficult and confusing situations we face in the world. The obedience of life flowing from that discernment makes of our lives a continual and "living sacrifice" that is acceptable and pleasing to God.

Paul then begins to offer more detailed guidance for relationships within the Christian community (verses 3-8). Considering that faith and the spiritual gifts are a result of God's grace, believers must judge themselves and their gifts humbly in relationship to the community. The metaphor of the body expresses the ideal of a diversity of gifts within a unity of faith. As "one body in Christ," the church is made up of many members who have no need to compete with one another, but who freely complement one another for the sake of the whole. Each member is given "gifts that differ according to the grace given to us." Offering a representative sample of these gifts and their functions, Paul emphasizes that they are not the possession of the members but are endowments to be used for ministry within the community.

Paul's remaining exhortations offer a description of the Christian life as a holy and living sacrifice to God. His list has many parallels with Jesus' teachings, especially the Sermon on the Mount. Love heads the list and penetrates the entire sequence. Paul first describes love within the Christian community (verses 9-13), and then love within the wider society (verses 14-21). Christian love is not shaped by the standards of the world or by our natural inclinations but by the power of God's Spirit transforming the mind and will of believers according to the standards of divine mercy lived by Jesus Christ.

Paul's advice on the love of Christians within the church is modeled on the affectionate love within families—the generous love of spouses and the patient care of siblings for one another. His counsel for Christian love within the wider world, however, clusters around his call for non-retaliation in the face of opposition and persecution. He guides us into a practical execution of Jesus' command to love our enemies (Matt 5:44; Luke 6:27). Through the teachings of the gospel and divine mercy at work within us, God is transforming us in the Spirit to receive, understand, and obey his radical teachings for life in the world. To bless our persecutors and not avenge our wrongs require the selflessness that only the power of God's love can bestow. The heart converted by divine mercy is able to discern God's will, to know what is "good and acceptable and perfect" (verse 2), and to "overcome evil with good" (verse 21) through union with the resurrected Lord and the power of his Spirit within.

Reflection and Discussion

- Why does Paul exhort believers in Christ to present their lives as a "living sacrifice" to God (verse 1)? What are the implications of living life as an offering to God?

- Every community has "gifts that differ according to the grace given to us." What are some of these diverse gifts within my family, group, or parish?

- What does Paul mean when he says, "Let love be genuine" (verse 9)? How can I tell when my love is "genuine" and when it is "conformed to this world" (verse 2)?

- Paul offers many marks of a merciful Christian in this passage. What can I do to put into practice one of his exhortations in my family, school, work, or church?

Prayer

God of divine mercy, you have given me the gift of your Spirit to renew my mind and convert my heart so that I can discern your will. Give me the humility to see my life in Christ as your gift and to love genuinely as Christ has loved me.

God, who is rich in mercy, out of the great love with which he loved us even when we were dead through our trespasses, made us alive together with Christ. EPH 2:4-5

Salvation by Grace through Faith

EPHESIANS 2:1-10 *¹You were dead through the trespasses and sins ²in which you once lived, following the course of this world, following the ruler of the power of the air, the spirit that is now at work among those who are disobedient. ³All of us once lived among them in the passions of our flesh, following the desires of flesh and senses, and we were by nature children of wrath, like everyone else. ⁴But God, who is rich in mercy, out of the great love with which he loved us ⁵even when we were dead through our trespasses, made us alive together with Christ—by grace you have been saved— ⁶and raised us up with him and seated us with him in the heavenly places in Christ Jesus, ⁷so that in the ages to come he might show the immeasurable riches of his grace in kindness toward us in Christ Jesus. ⁸For by grace you have been saved through faith, and this is not your own doing; it is the gift of God— ⁹not the result of works, so that no one may boast. ¹⁰For we are what he has made us, created in Christ Jesus for good works, which God prepared beforehand to be our way of life.*

An appreciation of God's unfathomable mercy toward us must begin with a realization of the depth of misery and alienation into which humanity has fallen through sin. Paul describes the plight of human life outside of the divine mercy we have received in Jesus Christ. Because we were spiritually dead, we were enslaved by three forces (verses 1-3). First, "the course of this world" captured us with a way of life that is contrary to and apart from God. Second, "the ruler of the power of the air," a title for Satan, held sway over us. The malign influence of demonic powers and their rebellious spirit held control over those who pitted themselves against God. And third, "the passions of our flesh," those instinctual desires distorted by sin that lead us to crave power, possessions, and pleasure, dominated human life. Under this condition of spiritual death there is no desire to relate one's life to God, and none of us can pull out of this morass with our own power.

Then, as if emerging out of the darkness, comes Paul's magnificent announcement: "But God, who is rich in mercy, out of the great love with which he loved us even when we were dead through our trespasses, made us alive together with Christ" (verses 4-5). The darkness of hopelessness and desperation has only made the light of God's merciful love shine more brightly. In contrast to the three forces that held us in spiritual death, Paul names three experiences that the believer shares in union with Christ. First, we are made "alive together with Christ." Second we are "raised up" with Christ. And third, we are "seated" or enthroned with Christ in the heavenly places (verses 5-6). Paul expresses the fact that we share these experiences intimately with Christ and thus with everyone else in the body of Christ. The life of Christ shines into our present life, already giving us a share in God's reign.

Our share in the resurrection and exaltation with Christ, as we experience it in this age and "in the ages to come," is a demonstration of "the immeasurable riches of his grace in kindness toward us in Christ Jesus" (verse 7). The mercy of God has already richly blessed us in Christ, yet our present experience is just a foretaste of the ongoing experience of God's mercy from age to age. Throughout the generations to come, the riches of God's mercy will be extended toward humanity through the church until the final age when all creation will be glorified in Christ.

Paul emphasizes that the overflowing blessings that God has bestowed upon us is a result of God's mercy upon undeserving humanity: "For by grace you have been saved through faith" (verse 8). Salvation is the coming together of God's grace and our faith. Divine grace is the life of God freely given to us. There is nothing we can do to earn or deserve this gracious gift of God. Faith is our reception of the good news of Christ and our personal trust in God. So, Paul notes that "no one may boast" because the new life we have received is all God's doing. It is up to us to open our hearts to God's gift, but "we are what he has made us" (verse 10). In God's mercy we have been given life in Jesus Christ, a way of life marked by "good works," the works of mercy.

Reflection and Discussion

- Paul effectively contrasts the experience of spiritual death with life in Christ. In what ways do you continue to feel the influence and draw of both realms?

- We are made alive with Christ, raised up with Christ, and seated with Christ. When did this reality begin for us? In what sense is it incomplete?

- "By grace you have been saved through faith." How does this phrase of Paul express the wonders of God's mercy toward us?

Prayer

O God, you are rich in mercy, and with great love you have raised us up to life with Christ. Thank you for rescuing me, your undeserving creature, from death and calling me to life. Thank you for your mercy.

Christ Jesus came into the world to save sinners—of whom I am the foremost. But for that very reason I received mercy.

1 TIM 1:15-16

New Birth through God's Mercy

1 TIMOTHY 1:12-17 *¹²I am grateful to Christ Jesus our Lord, who has strengthened me, because he judged me faithful and appointed me to his service, ¹³even though I was formerly a blasphemer, a persecutor, and a man of violence. But I received mercy because I had acted ignorantly in unbelief, ¹⁴and the grace of our Lord overflowed for me with the faith and love that are in Christ Jesus. ¹⁵The saying is sure and worthy of full acceptance, that Christ Jesus came into the world to save sinners—of whom I am the foremost. ¹⁶But for that very reason I received mercy, so that in me, as the foremost, Jesus Christ might display the utmost patience, making me an example to those who would come to believe in him for eternal life. ¹⁷To the King of the ages, immortal, invisible, the only God, be honor and glory forever and ever. Amen.*

1 PETER 1:3-12 *³Blessed be the God and Father of our Lord Jesus Christ! By his great mercy he has given us a new birth into a living hope through the resurrection of Jesus Christ from the dead, ⁴and into an inheritance that is imperishable, undefiled, and unfading, kept in heaven for you, ⁵who are being protected by the power of God through faith for a salvation ready to be revealed in the last time. ⁶In this you rejoice, even if now for a little while you have had to suffer various trials, ⁷so that the genuineness of your faith—being more precious than gold that, though* *perishable, is tested by fire—may be found to result in praise and glory and honor when Jesus Christ is revealed. [8]Although you have not seen him, you love him; and even though you do not see him now, you believe in him and rejoice with an indescribable and glorious joy, [9]for you are receiving the outcome of your faith, the salvation of your souls.*

[10]Concerning this salvation, the prophets who prophesied of the grace that was to be yours made careful search and inquiry, [11]inquiring about the person or time that the Spirit of Christ within them indicated when it testified in advance to the sufferings destined for Christ and the subsequent glory. [12]It was revealed to them that they were serving not themselves but you, in regard to the things that have now been announced to you through those who brought you good news by the Holy Spirit sent from heaven—things into which angels long to look!

Paul's message to Timothy describes how God's mercy worked in his own life, graciously bringing him from life as a blasphemer, persecutor, and man of violence, to new life in Christ. His words take the form of a personal testimony and thanksgiving to God. Paul is amazed that he received mercy in such abundance in relation to the enormity of his sin. With astonished gratitude, Paul explains, "The grace of our Lord overflowed for me with the faith and love that are in Christ Jesus" (1 Tim 1:14). Conversion and new life came for Paul in a full tide of divine mercy.

After offering his personal testimony about how God's grace flowed into his life, Paul recalls a saying that must have been commonly repeated in the early church: "Christ Jesus came into the world to save sinners" (1 Tim 1:15). He describes these words as "sure and worthy of full acceptance" because he has experienced the reality in his own life in an extraordinary way. That any sinner should receive God's mercy is remarkable, but for one who thought of himself as "the foremost" sinner, it stunned him with sheer wonder to recall it.

Paul says, "I received mercy" so that Christ could make him "an example" for others who might come to believe in Christ and receive eternal life (1 Tim 1:16). Paul is a primary exhibit for all other sinners. If God could give such mercy to him, given who he was and what he did, then there is hope for everyone. God's mercy is unlimited. With such gratitude and hope, Paul can only give honor and glory to the King of the ages (1 Tim 1:17).

The letter of Peter offers praise for what God has done "by his great mercy" (1 Pet 1:3). Solely because of God's gracious gift, we have been given "new birth" through the total triumph of Jesus Christ over death. The first result of this new life for believers is hope—a living hope that can no more fail than the living God who gives it. Our new birth into God's family makes us eligible for "an inheritance"—the fullness of salvation that is being kept for us to experience after the suffering of various trials (1 Pet 1:4-6).

The church addressed by Peter was undergoing suffering and persecution, the kinds of trials that are necessary for a mature and genuine faith. But faith that is tested and purified, like gold in the fire, will result in "praise, glory, and honor" when Jesus Christ is fully revealed in the last days (1 Peter 1:7). The members of the church addressed by Peter had never seen the Lord during his earthly life and will not have an opportunity of setting eyes on him, but that has not prevented them from becoming believers and committing their lives to him. Their love for the unseen Lord continues to grow, and his presence in their lives is real, so that they "rejoice with an indescribable and glorious joy" (1 Peter 1:8). This joy is God's merciful gift, a joy beyond human description that begins even in the midst of trials. It is a joy based on the assurance of faith, the confident trust of a believer in the fullness of salvation.

Our salvation begins when divine grace meets our faith at the moment of conversion; it grows within us through trials; and it finds its completion in the presence of our glorified Lord. This salvation is God's merciful gift to us—a gift for which prophets and even angels longed and searched (1 Peter 1:10-12). The Spirit of Christ inspired the prophets of old to speak about "the sufferings destined for Christ and the subsequent glory." God's plan for salvation was not fulfilled in their own days, but we are privileged to be living in the time when we can see the fullness of God's plan of salvation and rejoice in it.

Reflection and Discussion

- How does the experience of Paul demonstrate that God's mercy is unlimited?

- What are some of the similarities in how Paul and Peter give praise to God for divine mercy?

- In what ways, according to Peter, do trials and suffering deepen and mature our faith in Jesus Christ? How have I experienced this process in my own life?

- Why does God's great mercy, as described by Peter, evoke such unfailing hope and indescribable joy?

Prayer

King of the ages, immortal, invisible, the only God, to you be honor and glory forever and ever. The salvation you offer is the source of our unfailing hope and indescribable joy. Thank you for bestowing such mercy upon the world.

Has not God chosen the poor in the world to be rich in faith and to be heirs of the kingdom that he has promised to those who love him? JAMES 2:5

Mercy Triumphs over Judgment

JAMES 2:1-17 ¹*My brothers and sisters, do you with your acts of favoritism really believe in our glorious Lord Jesus Christ?* ²*For if a person with gold rings and in fine clothes comes into your assembly, and if a poor person in dirty clothes also comes in,* ³*and if you take notice of the one wearing the fine clothes and say, "Have a seat here, please," while to the one who is poor you say, "Stand there," or, "Sit at my feet,"* ⁴*have you not made distinctions among yourselves, and become judges with evil thoughts?* ⁵*Listen, my beloved brothers and sisters. Has not God chosen the poor in the world to be rich in faith and to be heirs of the kingdom that he has promised to those who love him?* ⁶*But you have dishonored the poor. Is it not the rich who oppress you? Is it not they who drag you into court?* ⁷*Is it not they who blaspheme the excellent name that was invoked over you?*

⁸*You do well if you really fulfill the royal law according to the scripture, "You shall love your neighbor as yourself."* ⁹*But if you show partiality, you commit sin and are convicted by the law as transgressors.* ¹⁰*For whoever keeps the whole law but fails in one point has become accountable for all of it.* ¹¹*For the one who said, "You shall not commit adultery," also said, "You shall not murder." Now if you do not commit adultery but if you murder, you have become a transgressor of the law.* ¹²*So speak and so act as those who are to be judged by the law of liberty.* ¹³*For judgment will be without mercy to anyone who has shown no mercy; mercy triumphs over judgment.*

¹⁴What good is it, my brothers and sisters, if you say you have faith but do not have works? Can faith save you? ¹⁵If a brother or sister is naked and lacks daily food, ¹⁶and one of you says to them, "Go in peace; keep warm and eat your fill," and yet you do not supply their bodily needs, what is the good of that? ¹⁷So faith by itself, if it has no works, is dead.

The life and teachings of Jesus bore witness to his undeniable commitment to the poor and outcasts. Jesus demonstrated obedience to the Torah of Israel, as exemplified in Leviticus 19:15-18, a portion of Israel's law that forbade partiality to the poor or deference to the rich, commanded that justice be done to the neighbor, forbade vengeance and grudges, and culminates in the command to "love your neighbor as yourself." Because Jesus embodied Israel's Torah by living with such loving care for the marginalized, James exhorts those to whom he writes to exhibit a similar mercy to those in need. If they truly believe in Jesus Christ, they must not show favoritism toward those who display wealth, influence, and attractiveness.

James presents an illustration of partiality based on realistic events within the Christian community (verses 2-4). The contrast in the way that the two persons—the person of influence and the poor person—are treated is designed to shock readers so that they will easily agree that such behavior is contrary to the way of life taught by the Torah and inspired by Jesus. He asks, "Has not God chosen the poor in the world to be rich in faith and to be heirs of the kingdom that he has promised to those who love him?" (verse 5). God's choice of the marginalized Hebrews enslaved in Egypt and Jesus' choice of the poor outcasts of his society demonstrate the fundamental option for the poor that God's people must demonstrate.

Yet James criticizes his audience: God has chosen the poor, but his audience has dishonored the poor (verse 6). Instead of embracing God's values, they continue to operate according to the standards of the world. In fact, James says, the wealthy and powerful exploit the poor and weak. When the poor need a loan, the rich give it to them for a price. When the poor cannot repay the loan, the rich drag them to court to foreclose. They set up society so that the poor get poorer and the rich get richer. Since God has chosen the poor to inherit the kingdom, those who refuse to imitate God's choice place themselves under God's judgment. Those who shame the poor in any way have placed themselves outside of God's will, and a community that dishonors the poor no longer acts on behalf of God.

James then urges the community he is addressing to "fulfill the royal law," that is, to follow the Torah as the expression of God's will (verse 8). Those who carry out God's will in obedience to Jesus' teachings inherit God's kingdom. Those who show partiality "commit sin" and show themselves to be transgressors of God's will (verse 9). James' exhortation that we keep "the whole law" does not require a scrupulous adherence to every detail of Scripture, but the orientation of our whole life to carrying out God's will in its entirety (verse 10). In this sense, according to James, showing contempt for the poor is equivalent to committing murder or adultery.

Above all, in light of God's judgment, we must show mercy. James reflects the teachings of Jesus: "For judgment will be without mercy to anyone who has shown no mercy" (verse 13). He adds, "Mercy triumphs over judgment." Those who practice mercy have no reason to fear the judgment of God. If we are merciful and judge the poor with mercy, we can stand before God with confidence when we are called to present our works on the last day. The Son of Man will invite those who have truly shown mercy toward the least of their brothers and sisters to enter the promised kingdom (Matt 25:34).

Faith must be completed with works of mercy. "Faith by itself, if it has no works, is dead" (verses 14-17). James again illustrates his words with an example. If our brothers or sisters are naked and lacking in daily food, and we offer a wishful remark and tell them we will pray for them, our faith is meaningless. The prophets raged against those who offered abundant sacrifices in the temple but neglected their social responsibilities toward the needy. "I desire mercy, not sacrifice," quoted Jesus from the prophet Hosea (Matt 9:13). A faith that is alive and real must demonstrate itself in works of mercy.

Reflection and Discussion

- What might be an example of discriminatory behavior today that would illustrate the same point James is making here?

- In what ways can a church take the wrong side among the rich and the poor? What happens to a Christian community when it takes on the characteristics of the wealthy and influential?

- What does James mean when he says, "Mercy triumphs over judgment"? Does this make you fearful or confident?

Prayer

Lord Jesus Christ, you urge me to love my neighbor and to show mercy to those in need. Enliven my faith in you so that it overflows with compassion for the poor and works of mercy toward the brother or sister who lacks food, clothing, shelter, or companionship.

Love has been perfected among us in this: that we may have boldness on the day of judgment, because as he is, so are we in this world. 1 JOHN 4:17

We Love Because He First Loved Us

1 JOHN 4:7-21 *⁷Beloved, let us love one another, because love is from God; everyone who loves is born of God and knows God. ⁸Whoever does not love does not know God, for God is love. ⁹God's love was revealed among us in this way: God sent his only Son into the world so that we might live through him. ¹⁰In this is love, not that we loved God but that he loved us and sent his Son to be the atoning sacrifice for our sins. ¹¹Beloved, since God loved us so much, we also ought to love one another. ¹²No one has ever seen God; if we love one another, God lives in us, and his love is perfected in us.*

¹³By this we know that we abide in him and he in us, because he has given us of his Spirit. ¹⁴And we have seen and do testify that the Father has sent his Son as the Savior of the world. ¹⁵God abides in those who confess that Jesus is the Son of God, and they abide in God. ¹⁶So we have known and believe the love that God has for us.

God is love, and those who abide in love abide in God, and God abides in them. ¹⁷Love has been perfected among us in this: that we may have boldness on the day of judgment, because as he is, so are we in this world. ¹⁸There is no fear in love, but perfect love casts out fear; for fear has to do with punishment, and whoever fears has not reached perfection in love. ¹⁹We love because he first loved us. ²⁰Those who say, "I love God," and hate their brothers or sisters, are liars; for those who do not love a brother or sister whom they have seen, cannot love God whom they have not seen. [21] *The commandment we have from him is this: those who love God must love their brothers and sisters also.*

Love has its origins in God. Only because we have experienced divine love are we capable of love. Love is how God manifests the divine presence to us because, in fact, "God is love" (verses 7-8). But this love that is of God is not just any love, as we casually use the word. Divine love is self-giving, compassionate, faithful, undeserved, unearned, overflowing love. And the flow of this love as it streams into our lives is divine mercy.

This God who is love has revealed this merciful love in concrete, historical events—in sending his only Son into the world and, supremely, in his atoning sacrifice for our sins (verses 9-10). This is the definitive expression of love, the true standard of authentic love. This love that God has shown us becomes our mandate to love in this same way: "Since God loved us so much, we also ought to love one another" (verse 11). Our loving becomes, then, the means God uses to live in us and to perfect his love within us (verse 12).

As God's love is not an abstraction but consists in God giving his Son for us, so our love is not merely an attitude or an emotion but consists of tangible actions and works of mercy. Even though "no one has ever seen God," God's presence can be felt and truly experienced at work within the world when we love one another. Our tangible love for other people not only demonstrates the flow of divine love within us but also makes credible the message of God's love in witness to the world.

Through the presence of the Holy Spirit, we live in a mutually indwelling relationship with God (verse 13). "Those who abide in love abide in God, and God abides in them" (verse 16). In this way, divine love is perfected within us, both as individuals and as Christ's church. This quality of divine love working within us casts out fear, so that we have no reason to be afraid of God's judgment (verses 17-18). Whatever fear we may have simply indicates that our transformation in love is incomplete. As we allow God's love to complete its work in us, there is no more room for fear. We can have deep trust in God and great confidence in our eternal future.

Finally, John affirms that we can only love the unseen God by loving other people. Those who claim to love God are liars if, at the same time, they hate their brothers or sisters (verse 20). Since it is easier to love a brother or sister whom we have seen than to love the unseen God, we cannot love God if we do not love our highly visible brothers and sisters.

Reflection and Discussion

- In what ways is God's love different than the ways we commonly use the word in our culture? Why is the cross the surest sign of divine love?

- John wrote, "We love because he first loved us" (verse 19). Why is it necessary for human beings to receive love before they are able to give love? How does my experience prove this to be so?

- John tells us that God's love is perfected within us as we love one another (verse 12). What experiences have led to the perfecting of divine love within me?

Prayer

Merciful God, you manifest yourself to us through love, and you show that love most fully through the cross of your Son. Continue to perfect your love within me, helping me to offer that love to others.

"He will wipe every tear from their eyes. Death will be no more; mourning and crying and pain will be no more, for the first things have passed away." REV 21:4

God's Final and Eternal Act of Mercy

REVELATION 21:1-7 *¹Then I saw a new heaven and a new earth; for the first heaven and the first earth had passed away, and the sea was no more. ²And I saw the holy city, the new Jerusalem, coming down out of heaven from God, prepared as a bride adorned for her husband. ³And I heard a loud voice from the throne saying,*

"See, the home of God is among mortals.
He will dwell with them as their God;
they will be his peoples,
and God himself will be with them;
⁴he will wipe every tear from their eyes.
Death will be no more;
mourning and crying and pain will be no more,
for the first things have passed away."

⁵And the one who was seated on the throne said, "See, I am making all things new." Also he said, "Write this, for these words are trustworthy and true." ⁶Then he said to me, "It is done! I am the Alpha and the Omega, the beginning and the end. To the thirsty I will give water as a gift from the spring of the water of life. ⁷Those who conquer will inherit these things, and I will be their God and they will be my children."

REVELATION 22:1-5 *¹Then the angel showed me the river of the water of life, bright as crystal, flowing from the throne of God and of the Lamb ²through the middle of the street of the city. On either side of the river is the tree of life with its twelve kinds of fruit, producing its fruit each month; and the leaves of the tree are for the healing of the nations. ³Nothing accursed will be found there anymore. But the throne of God and of the Lamb will be in it, and his servants will worship him; ⁴they will see his face, and his name will be on their foreheads. ⁵And there will be no more night; they need no light of lamp or sun, for the Lord God will be their light, and they will reign forever and ever.*

T
hese final chapters of the Bible express God's full and final demonstration of mercy toward us, an eternal act of merciful love in God's own presence. Our ultimate destiny is a condition far beyond anything we can imagine and far above anything our humanity could ever achieve. For us to experience the fullness of eternal life with God is utter gift, pure mercy.

The last scenes of the Book of Revelation are the writer's attempt to express the beauty and joy of God's new creation. This new heaven and new earth are creation perfected by their Creator. Human language is incapable of expressing, and human imagination is incapable of perceiving, the perfection of God's reign over creation. As Paul wrote, "What no eye has seen, nor ear heard, nor the human heart conceived, what God has prepared for those who love him" (1 Cor 2:9).

These verses employ a variety of images to evoke the goodness and splendor of God that permeates the resurrected life. It is like a new, perfected Jerusalem in which all can live (21:2), like the beauty of a bride prepared for her wedding, as fresh and new as water from a spring (21:6). Its wonder is due to the fact that God dwells with his people. God makes his home with humanity and cares for his people in all their needs: "[God] will wipe every tear from their eyes. Death will be no more; mourning and crying and pain will be no more (21:4). God's people will finally experience the fullness of life, joy, and love.

Yet, this fullness of God's will for creation is not reserved only for some distant future. God declares, "See, I am making all things new" (21:5). The present tense indicates that God is already making things new right now. We have already begun to experience God's presence, divine comfort, and new life. To be sure, with the coming of Jesus, God has already begun a new creation in his Son and in all those who are united with him. Even if our experience of God's presence is often faint and fragmentary now, we can find consolation in this vision because we know that what we have experienced dimly will embrace us completely.

The fullest result of God's mercy toward us is salvation, the completion of our redemption. It is symbolized by Paradise restored, with a river flowing through the city of God and the tree of life that grew in Eden blooming in its streets and bearing twelve kinds of fruit (22:1-2). In the midst of this perfected creation is the throne of God and of Christ the Lamb. There we will worship God and see his face. We will be with God, know him completely, and trust in him. God's name will be on our foreheads, signifying that we belong to God and are precious to him (22:3-4). To be a resident of this city means being with God, in such an intimate way that human language falters when trying to express its wonders.

This vision of God's mercy, completed for us and for all creation, shows us what God has in store for us, the fulfillment of all the hopes of Scripture. The final words of God in the Bible are words of hope, mercy, and love. Beyond all the tears and pain of humanity's history, men and women experience the fullness of God's kingdom and "they will reign forever and ever" (22:5).

Reflection and Discussion

- Which of the many images in these passages speak most clearly to me about the mercy God has in store for the future?

- What will it be like to live without pain, sin, fear, or death, and with the full presence of God? What glimpses has God given me of the joys that await me?

- The new creation, God's renewal of the heavens and the earth, has begun in Jesus Christ. How can I unite my life more fully with his?

- In what ways has understanding and reflecting on God's mercy throughout this study made an impact on the way I live my life?

Prayer

Merciful and loving God, you have created me and you can make me new. Move my heart to long for your kingdom and to anticipate the good things you have in store for me.

SUGGESTIONS FOR FACILITATORS, GROUP SESSION 6

1. Welcome group members and make any final announcements or requests.

2. You may want to pray this prayer as a group
   Lord God, you are rich in mercy. You have rescued us from death through the cross of your Son, raised us to life with him, and given us the gift of your Spirit. Your mercy is the source of our unfailing hope and indescribable joy. We praise you for bestowing such mercy upon the world. As you perfect your love within us, help us to offer that love to others through works of mercy toward those who lack food, clothing, shelter, or companionship. As we study your word, bless us with compassion, generosity, and love for one another.

3. Ask one or more of the following questions:
   - How has this study of God's mercy deepened your life in Christ?
   - In what way has this study challenged you the most?

4. Discuss lessons 25 through 30. Choose one or more of the questions for reflection and discussion from each lesson to discuss as a group.

5. Ask the group if they would like to study another in the Threshold Bible Study series. Discuss the topic and dates, and make a decision among those interested. Ask the group members to suggest people they would like to invite to participate in the next study series.

6. Ask the group to discuss the insights that stand out most from this study over the past six weeks.

7. Conclude by praying aloud the following prayer or another of your own choosing:
   Holy Spirit of the living God, you inspired the writers of the Scriptures and you have guided our study during these weeks. Continue to deepen our love for the word of God in the holy Scriptures, and draw us more deeply into the heart of Jesus. Thank you for your merciful, gracious, steadfast, and faithful love.

Ordering Additional Studies

AVAILABLE TITLES IN THIS SERIES INCLUDE...

TWENTY
THIRD
PUBLICATIONS

TO CHECK AVAILABILITY OR FOR A DESCRIPTION
OF EACH STUDY, VISIT OUR WEBSITE AT
www.ThresholdBibleStudy.com
OR CALL US AT **1-800-321-0411**